CRIME SCENE
PROCESSING AND
INVESTIGATION

WORKBOOK

CRIME SCENE PROCESSING AND INVESTIGATION
WORKBOOK

CHRISTINE R. RAMIREZ
CASIE PARISH-FISHER

CRC Press
Taylor & Francis Group
Boca Raton   London   New York

CRC Press is an imprint of the
Taylor & Francis Group, an **informa** business

CRC Press
Taylor & Francis Group
6000 Broken Sound Parkway NW, Suite 300
Boca Raton, FL 33487-2742

International Standard Book Number: 978-1-4398-4970-5 (Paperback)

Library of Congress Cataloging-in-Publication Data

Parish-Fisher, Casie L.
    Crime scene processing and investigation workbook / Casie L. Parish-Fisher, Christine R. Ramirez.
        p. cm.
    Includes bibliographical references and index.
    ISBN 978-1-4398-4970-5 (pbk. : alk. paper)
    1. Crime scene searches. 2. Criminal investigation. 3. Evidence, Criminal. I. Ramirez, Christine R. II. Title.

HV8073.P29 2012
363.25'2--dc23   2011037845

**Visit the Taylor & Francis Web site at
http://www.taylorandfrancis.com**

**and the CRC Press Web site at
http://www.crcpress.com**

Dedication

For the previous, current, and future seekers of truth

Contents

Chapter 3.   Actions of the Initial Responding Officer 33

Chapter 4.   Processing Methodology 37

Acknowledgments

The creation of this workbook is a direct result of the support and encouragement of Ross Gardner. Thank you, Ross, for your trust in us. Many thanks also to Rachel E. Martin for creating the artwork for this workbook. You took scribbled drawings on paper and turned them into our exact visions. Your talent and skill are remarkable.

I could not have had a better partner in this project than Casie Parish-Fisher. This workbook was born, in part, out of your desire to create a tool to benefit your students, our future forensics professionals. I am proud to be your colleague and fortunate to be your friend. I look forward to our next adventure.

I would be remiss if I did not acknowledge the hard working, dedicated crime scene investigators and detectives of the Montgomery County Sheriff's Office. I consider these men and women to be more than my colleagues. They are my family. I offer special gratitude to Capt. Peggy Frankhouser from whom I have learned a great deal. One of the greatest lessons learned is that our foundation should be firm and our shoulders sturdy as those who come after us will stand upon them. I thank you, for I stand on your shoulders. It is my hope that I am sturdy enough for our future practitioners to someday stand on mine.

Without the sacrifices and fortitude of my parents, Carlos and Rose Ramirez, this workbook would not have been possible. Thank you for teaching me that with faith and hard work anything is possible and achievable. To my sister, Nicole, your strength and courage are inspiring. William Eric, my husband, your support has been constant and your patience endless. You have believed in me not only during the challenge of this endeavor, but always. And to William Hewitt, my son, you are and always will be my sunshine.

Christine R. Ramirez

I thank the following people for their support and dedication:

Christine Ramirez for your unwavering support, creative ideas, and ability to me keep going when we were both exhausted. You are a wonderful colleague and friend and I hope this is the first of many good works to come.

To my wonderful husband, Chris Fisher, for being supportive and encouraging throughout this entire process. I couldn't have done it without you.

My parents, Butch and Charlotte Parish, and brother, Chase, who have always been encouraging and supportive of all my goals and dreams.

Dr. David Horton, professor and chair of the baccalaureate programs in Criminology, Criminal Justice and Forensic Science at St. Edward's University; Emily Bowers, coworker and friend; Trisha Castillo and Ashley McTiernan, students at St. Edward's University for your critical review of the workbook.

Dean Brenda Vallance and all the faculty and staff at St. Edward's University for your encouragement and unwavering support of this work.

Kent Christianson, for taking a young college student at Baylor University under your wing and teaching and supporting me through my undergraduate and graduate career. Col. Frank Hillson, for your inspiring lectures and literature reviews during my undergraduate career at Baylor University, I never looked at a book the same way again.

All of you have played an important role leading up to this point in my life. I couldn't be here without you all.

Casie L. Parish-Fisher

Authors

Christine R. Ramirez is the coordinator of the Texas Forensic Science Academy within the Texas A&M University System's Texas Engineering Extension Service in College Station, Texas. She is an active instructor of crime scene investigation, evidence processing, friction ridge development, and bloodstain pattern analysis. She has developed forensic science courses and served as a subject matter expert for forensic science training manuals. Ms. Ramirez served as the senior crime scene investigator in the crime laboratory of one of the largest sheriff's offices in Texas. She currently holds a Master Peace Officer license from the state of Texas, with seventeen years of investigative experience. She is a Certified Senior Crime Scene Analyst by the International Association for Identification and is a court qualified expert in bloodstain pattern analysis and latent print examination. She graduated from Sam Houston State University with a bachelor of science degree in Criminal Justice. Ms. Ramirez is a member of the International Association for Identification, Texas Division of the International Association for Identification, and International Association of Bloodstain Pattern Analysts.

Casie L. Parish-Fisher is currently assistant professor of forensic science in the Bachelor of Science Degree Program at St. Edward's University, Austin, Texas. She graduated from Baylor University with a bachelor of science degree in forensic science. She completed her master's of science degree in DNA profiling at the University of Central Lancashire, Preston, England, and is currently matriculating on her PhD in research topics relating to DNA analysis. She is coeditor of a sui generis anthology titled *Pioneering Research in Forensic Science* (Lewiston-Queenston-Lampeter: Edwin Mellen Press, 2009) with colleagues from St. Edward's University, Dr. David M. Horton and instructor Michelle Y. Richter. She is a member of the International Association for Identification and the Texas Division of the International Association for Identification where she is a member of the board of directors and serves on the program committee, the host committee, and as chair of the student membership committee.

Key Terms

CSI effect
Evidence
Testimonial evidence
Physical evidence
Predictable effects
Unpredictable effects
Transitory effects
Relational details
Functional details

Learning Outcomes

1. Discuss what is meant by the "interpretive value of evidence."
2. Understand the CSI effect and its effects on society.
3. Describe physical and testimonial evidence.

1-1: Evaluating the Interpretive Value of Evidence

Objective

- Review crime scene material and identify key evidence. Once identified, evaluate the evidence and surrounding clues by using the five contexts of evidence described in the *Concept Overview*.

Materials

- Writing utensil

Concept Overview

The value of evidence is more than its presence at a crime scene. The context in which an item is found is sometimes more valuable than the item itself. It is up to the first responding officers and crime scene personnel to be studious of the crime scene and observe conditions that may be invaluable to solving a case.

When considering the context of evidence, "Rynearson and Chisum offered that such context might manifest itself in a number of ways." They classified these manifestations as:

- Predictable effects: regular changes one would expect to see at the scene or in evidence. Example: Insect activity at a homicide scene.
- Unpredictable effects: unexpected changes one would not expect to see at a crime scene. This is especially disastrous to an investigation as it could lead to the misinterpretation of the scene. Example: The altering of the crime scene by crime scene personnel.
- Transitory effects: fleeting changes within a crime scene. Example: The smoke from a burning cigarette.
- Relational details: rely on the ability of personnel to properly place items within a crime scene. These details help to establish a relationship among items at the scene. Example: Recognition of a void pattern on a wall with blood spatter.
- Functional details: concern themselves with the operating conditions of items at the scene. Example: a nonfunctional wrist watch found on a victim.

Procedure

1. Evaluate scene photographs.
2. Complete the *Evaluation Worksheet*.
3. Complete the Post Lab Questions.

Evaluation Worksheet

PHOTOGRAPH: _____

Item	Context	Justification

Evaluation Worksheet

PHOTOGRAPH: _____

Item	Context	Justification

PHOTOGRAPH: _____

Item	Context	Justification

Evaluation Worksheet

PHOTOGRAPH: _____

Item	Context	Justification

Post Lab Questions

1. Why is it important to observe the context of evidence at a scene?
2. Give two examples of transitory effects.
3. Is testimonial evidence more valuable than physical evidence? Explain.
4. In evaluating the photographs, what was the most difficult part?
5. Review the following list of items and notate the context of evidence. Be sure to justify your answer. (Make no assumptions as to the time or type of crime.)

(More than one context could apply, if so, explain your answer.)

   a. Livor mortis in a body.
   b. A home security alarm that is not activated but the door is open.
   c. A handgun under the victim's body.
   d. The smell of perfume in a male victim's bathroom.
   e. Police clearing a home with no regard to evidence.
   f. A dirty mattress impression on the floor of a basement.
   g. A jammed gun.

1-2: CSI Effect

Objectives

- Describe the CSI effect.
- Identify several of the basic objectives used to meet the goals of law enforcement.

- Identify and describe examples of physical evidence and testimonial evidence.
- Identify and describe several scene context classifications.
- Explain how the CSI effect could affect trial jury members.

Materials

- Paper (for note taking)
- Writing utensil

Concept Overview

Law enforcement has two basic objectives: crime prevention and preservation of peace, and protection of life, property, and personal liberty. These are accomplished through several goals:

1. Crime prevention: This includes the actions and efforts designed to keep crime from occurring. Community programs, youth programs, and proactive directed patrol are all good examples of crime prevention.

2. Crime repression: When crime prevention fails, law enforcement must then seek to repress the crime that is occurring. Actively pursuing the assailants leads to more apprehensions and enhanced community security.

3. Regulating noncriminal conduct or patrolling: Law enforcement must also work to control the general area and its occupants. Obeying city ordinances and traffic regulations helps to prevent chaos.

4. Provision of services: A police officer's main priority is the safety and well-being of its citizens. This is the largest area of service an officer may encounter and includes everything from changing a pedestrian's tire to looking for a lost child.

5. Protection of personal liberty: Police must exercise a directive to protect citizens from unwarranted police interference of their personal liberties. Officers must also act to control their own actions and abide by the Constitution and the laws of their governing states. This is an act of obeying the law without obstructing the law.

Evidence is used to prove an alleged matter of fact. Testimonial evidence is collected through an interview or interrogation of a witness, suspect, or other various subjects involved with the scene. Physical evidence takes the form of specific items found within the scene. They are often collected and submitted to a laboratory for further analysis and possibly presented in court. Whether submitted to a laboratory or not, all physical evidence should be documented through photography and sketching at the scene. Both types of evidence are crucial to an investigation, allowing investigators to fully reconstruct what may have occurred.

The *CSI effect* is the false or exaggerated perception of forensic science techniques by the general public, and it influences opinions of the public. The term is most commonly used in reference to jurors who expect flashy scientific techniques in trials. The trend started with early criminal investigation shows such as *Quincy, M.E.* and began to explode in the late 1990s and early 2000 with the popularity of crime dramas such as *CSI*. Noticeable effects of the television shows include increased casework in criminal laboratories and the dramatic increase in the number of forensic science programs at colleges and universities. Although the shows are entertaining, they have been criticized for failing to portray forensic techniques accurately and misleading students concerning the actual work conducted. It is also possible the shows aid criminals by depicting methods of evidence disposal and destruction, thus making it more difficult for law enforcement to solve crimes.

Procedure

1. Read literature concerning the CSI effect.
2. View the instructor-provided presentation.

3. During viewing, take notes concerning the context of the following within the presentation:

- One or more of the basic objectives used to meet the goals of law enforcement:
    - crime prevention
    - crime repression
    - regulation of noncriminal conduct
    - provision of services
    - protection of personal liberty
- Examples of physical evidence and testimonial evidence, if any.
- Examples of scene context classifications:
    - predictable effects
    - unpredictable effects
    - transitory effects
    - relational details
- functional details

4. Complete the *Evaluation Worksheets.*

5. Complete the Post Lab Questions.

Evaluation Worksheet

Law Enforcement Objective	Plot Depiction
Crime Prevention	
Crime Repression	
Noncriminal Conduct	
Provision of Services	
Protection of Personal Liberty	

Evaluation Worksheet

Physical Evidence	Testimonial Evidence
1.	1.
2.	2.
3.	3.
4.	4.
5.	5.
6.	6.
7.	7.
8.	8.
9.	9.
10.	10.

Evaluation Worksheet

Scene Context Classifications	Plot Depiction
Predictable: Regular changes one would expect to see at a crime scene	
Unpredictable: Unexpected changes one would not expect to see at a crime scene	
Transitory: Fleeting changes	
Relational: Establishment of relationship between items at a crime scene	
Functional: Whether items within the scene are working properly or not	

Post Lab Questions

1. What is the CSI effect?
2. How could the CSI effect affect trial jury members?
3. Why is it important to understand the short falls of television shows?
4. How could the shows aid criminal activity?
5. Give an example of how a police officer can violate the law while on duty.
6. What are the two types of evidence? Why is it helpful to have both types?

Works Cited

Gardner, Ross M. *Practical Crime Scene Processing and Investigation.* Boca Raton, FL: CRC Press, 2005.

Lovgren, Stefan. "'CSI Effect' Is Mixed Blessing for Real Crime Labs." *National Geographic News*, September 23, 2004: 1–3.

Schweitzer N. J., and Michael J. Saks. "The CSI Effect: Popular Fiction About Forensic Science Affects the Public's Expectations About Real Forensic Science." *Jurimetrics*, 2007: 357–364.

Chapter 2

The Nature of Physical Evidence

Key Terms

Class characteristics
Cross contamination
Individual characteristics
Individualization
Latent print
Locard's principle of exchange
Dermis
Epidermis
Loop
Whorl
Arch
Minutiae
Rolled impressions
Plain impressions
Friction ridge skin
Positive control
Negative control
False positive
Mechanical fit

Learning Outcomes

1. Understand the different types of evidence that may be present at a crime scene.
2. Define class and individual characteristics.
3. Discuss contamination issues that may occur at a crime scene.
4. Understand the importance of Locard's exchange theory.
5. Demonstrate the ability to use mechanical fit.

2-1: Identifying Characteristics of Evidence

Objectives

- Identify the categories in which evidence can be classified.
- Review examples of evidence and identify whether the characteristics for each are class or individual.

Materials

- Paper
- Writing utensil

Concept Overview

Evidence recognition is a key component in crime scene processing. It is important for crime scene personnel to understand the value associated with the items collected at a scene.

Evidence is generally divided into items that exhibit class characteristics and those that exhibit individual characteristics. Class characteristics are characteristics or traits of an item that are unique to a specific group. The traits or characteristics are not individualizing. Examples of class characteristics are a shoeprint left by a female who wore size 8 shoes or a hair that came from a Hispanic male. Individual characteristics are traits or characteristics on an item that are specific or unique to that item. Examples of individual characteristics are the appearance and locations of tears, gouges, and cuts in a shoe print left behind at a crime scene that are the same as those on the shoe collected from the suspect. Individualization is established by linking all traits or characteristics on a specific item through examination or experimentation and either excluding or concluding that it originated from the crime scene.

There are several different disciplines of forensic science that can be used to analyze evidence. They are:

Serological/Biological:	Evidence that is associated with the human body and is used in DNA analysis. These types of items could yield both class and individual characteristics. Examples: bone, blood, semen, skin (epithelial cells), saliva.
Fingerprints:	Fingerprints are the most common type of evidence sought at a crime scene. The ridge detail and minutiae, located on the hands or feet of a person, yield individual characteristics.
Trace Evidence:	Trace evidence includes several different types of evidence including hairs/fibers, glass, paints/polymers, soil, and gunshot residue.

Hairs are a common form of trace evidence. Hairs can be distinguished by species, the general location on the body, and in cases of humans, by the general race (Caucasian, Negroid, and Mongoloid). Examination of the hair follicle includes its diameter, scales, medulla, pigment, and cortex. Hair generally exhibits class characteristics. However, in rare instances hair may exhibit individual characteristics.

Fibers, like hairs, are categorized by the originating source. They may be manufactured, naturally occurring, or synthetic. A variety of microscopes are used to examine fibers. Fibers generally exhibit class characteristics.

Glass is typically placed into three basic categories: glass type determinations, direction of force determinations, and sequence of force determinations. Type determinations evaluate known and unknown pieces of glass and try to determine if they have originated from a common source. Direction of force determinations assess the radial fractures present in the first concentric ring in an effort to conclude from which direction force was applied. Sequence of force determination evaluates conditions where multiple bullet defects are located in close proximity on the glass. When this occurs, it is necessary to note where the radial fractures meet and terminate. This will possibly help establish a sequence or order to the shots. Glass exhibits class characteristics.

Paints and polymers are encountered in a broad range of crime scenes. Paint is manufactured in a wide variety of types for different functions. Aside from color, or basic type (latex, enamel, semi-gloss, etc.), the chemical composition or ingredients of the paint may offer a means of discrimination. Paint samples are the iconic form of trace evidence since there is rarely any left behind at a crime scene. Paint can exhibit both class and individual characteristics.

Soils are a complex mixture of organic and inorganic compounds and can vary significantly in small areas. Examiners look for environmental contamination or unique environmental settings that can help isolate the sample's approximate location. Soil evidence is a good example of a class characteristic.

Gunshot residue (GSR) is discharged from a firearm and it contains significant amounts of both burned and unburned residue. The residues can be tested a variety of ways both at crime scenes and in the laboratory. GSR exhibits class characteristics.

Firearms/Ballistics: Firearms evidence contains both class and individual characteristics. Firearms analysis involves the examination of weapons and any expended shell casings, bullets, or cartridges. These combined efforts aim to associate each item with the other, ultimately leading to an identification of a weapon and its discharge.

Tool mark: Tool-mark evidence presents both class and individual characteristics. Tool marks are formed by the interaction of a tool with the crime scene. Three categories of marks are generally used. These include striations, compressions, and saw and drill markings. Striation marks are made when the tool comes into contact with an area and is slid against the target surface. A comparison mark occurs when a tool is forced onto a soft material. Saw and drill marks occur when the tool is actually used on the target surface.

Impression: Impression evidence manifests itself at a crime scene in a variety of forms. Shoe and tire marks, bite marks, tool marks (tools used on a malleable material), and plastic fingerprints (fingerprints that are left in a soft medium) are all good examples of impression evidence. Evidence of this nature can also be found as three-dimensional impressions (impression located in soft dirt) or two-dimensional impressions (shoe mark is deposited in grease on a hardwood surface). Impression evidence can be classified as having both class and individual characteristics.

Chemical: Chemical evidence is a unique form of evidence. Two types of analyses are generally conducted: drug analysis and toxicological analysis.

Drug analysis is preformed on items collected from individuals. For example, a bag of blue tablets is found in the trunk of a car. It would be necessary to determine if the pills were in fact a controlled substance.

Toxicological analysis is performed when evidence is taken from an individual in the form of bodily fluids; the fluids are then subjected to analysis. For example, a person is pulled over for erratic driving and a court order is issued to have his blood drawn. The results of the blood analysis would determine whether the person was over the legal limit. Chemical evidence can be classified as having both class and individual characteristics.

When handling evidence it is important to limit contamination. Contamination is the accidental transfer of biological or chemical components into an area. Cross contamination is directly associated with Locard's exchange theory. The theory states that when two objects come in contact with each other, trace elements of each of the items are transferred one to the other. It is important to wear personal protective equipment (PPE) such as gloves, masks, and booties to prevent this from occurring.

Procedure

1. Review all items presented.
2. Record on the *Evaluation Worksheet* what the item is, whether the item has class or individual characteristics, and provide a short explanation justifying your decision.
3. Complete the Post Lab Questions.

Evaluation Worksheet

PHOTOGRAPH: _____

Class Characteristic	Individual Characteristic	Justification

PHOTOGRAPH: _____

Class Characteristic	Individual Characteristic	Justification

PHOTOGRAPH: _____

Class Characteristic	Individual Characteristic	Justification

PHOTOGRAPH: _____

Class Characteristic	Individual Characteristic	Justification

PHOTOGRAPH: _____

Class Characteristic	Individual Characteristic	Justification

PHOTOGRAPH: _____

Class Characteristic	Individual Characteristic	Justification

PHOTOGRAPH: _____

Class Characteristic	Individual Characteristic	Justification

PHOTOGRAPH: _____

Class Characteristic	Individual Characteristic	Justification

PHOTOGRAPH: _____

Class Characteristic	Individual Characteristic	Justification

PHOTOGRAPH: _____

Class Characteristic	Individual Characteristic	Justification

Post Lab Questions

1. Give an evidentiary example for each of the following categories:

   Biological:
   Impression:
   Chemical:
   Firearms:

2. Why is it important to have a general understanding of the nature of evidence?
3. List three ways one could prevent contamination at a crime scene.
4. What is biological evidence? Why is it important?
5. How are drugs and toxicology the same? How are they different?

2-2: Evidence Processing

Objectives

- Identify the processes which specific items of evidence subjected.
- Review examples of evidence and identify what type of analysis should occur.

Materials

- Paper
- Writing utensil

Concept Overview

Evidence recognition is a key component in crime scene processing. It is also equally important to understand the processes associated with various types of evidentiary items. It is not uncommon for items to undergo multiple types of analysis to maximize their value to the investigation.

There are several different disciplines of forensic science that can be used to analyze evidence. They are:

Serological/DNA:	Evidence that is associated with the human body and is used in DNA analysis. Examples: bone, blood, semen, skin (epithelial cells), saliva.
Fingerprints:	Fingerprints are the most common type of evidence sought at a crime scene. The ridge detail and minutiae, located on the hands or feet of a person, yield individual characteristics.
Trace Evidence:	Trace examiners review a variety of evidentiary items. Trace items include hairs/fibers, glass, paints/polymers, soil, and gunshot residue.
	Hairs are a common form of trace evidence. Hairs can be distinguished by species, the general location on the body, and in cases of humans, by the general race (Caucasian, Negroid, and Mongoloid). Examination of the hair follicle includes its diameter, scales, medulla, pigment, and cortex. Hair generally exhibits class characteristics. However, in rare instances hair may exhibit individual characteristics.

Fibers, like hairs, are categorized by the originating source. They may be manufactured, naturally occurring, or synthetic. A variety of microscopes are used to examine fibers. Fibers generally exhibit class characteristics.

Glass is typically placed into three basic categories: glass type determinations, direction of force determinations, and sequence of force determinations. Type determinations evaluate known and unknown pieces of glass to determine if they originate from a common source. Direction of force determinations assess the radial fractures present in the first concentric ring in an effort to conclude from which direction force was applied. Sequence of force determination evaluates conditions where multiple bullet defects are located in close proximity on the glass. When this occurs, it is necessary to note where the radial fractures meet and terminate. This will possibly help establish a sequence or order to the shots. Glass exhibits class characteristics.

Paints and polymers are encountered in a broad range of crime scenes. Paint is manufactured in a wide variety of types for different functions. Aside from color, or basic type (latex, enamel, semigloss, etc.), the chemical composition or ingredients of the paint may offer a means of discrimination. Paint samples are the iconic forms of trace evidence since there is rarely any left behind at a crime scene. Paint can exhibit both class and individual characteristics.

Soils are complex mixtures of organic and inorganic compounds, and can vary significantly in small areas. Examiners look for environmental contamination or unique environmental settings that can help isolate the sample's approximate location. Soil evidence is a good example of a class characteristic.

Gunshot residue (GSR) is discharged from a firearm and contains significant amounts of both burned and unburned residue. The residues can be tested in a variety of ways both at crime scenes and in the laboratory. GSR exhibits class characteristics.

Firearms/Ballistics/Tool Marks:

Firearms analysis involves the examination of weapons and any expended shell casings, bullets, or cartridges. These combined efforts aim to associate one item with another, ultimately leading to identification of a weapon and its discharge.

Firearms examiners, in many cases, also conduct tool-mark analysis. Tool-mark evidence presents both class and individual characteristics. Tool marks are formed by the interaction of a tool with the crime scene. Three categories of marks are generally used: striations, compressions, and saw and drill markings. Striation marks are made when the tool comes in contact with an area and is slid against the target surface. A comparison mark occurs when a tool is forced onto a soft material. Saw and drill marks occur when the tool is actually used on the target surface.

Drug Analysis:

Drug analysis is preformed on items that are collected from individuals. For example, a bag of blue tablets is found in the trunk of a car. It would be necessary to determine if the pills were in fact a controlled substance.

Toxicology:

Toxicological analysis is performed when evidence is taken from an individual in the form of bodily fluids; the fluids are then subjected to analysis. For example, a person is pulled over for erratic driving and a court order is issued to have his blood drawn. The results of the blood analysis would determine whether the person was over the legal limit. Chemical evidence can be classified as having both class and individual characteristics.

Questioned Documents: Questioned document examiners examine all documents. Documents are defined as any fixed methods of communication between two or more persons. Many examiners are not only trained in handwriting analysis but also in computer forensic techniques that allow them to examine files contained in computer databases. Examples of document evidence include but are not limited to fake driver licenses, forged birth certificates, e-mail communication, suicide notes, etc.

Establishing evidentiary value is an important role for a crime scene technician and for an investigator. It is important to view all items for their significance in the ability to aid an investigation.

Procedure

1. Review all items presented.
2. Record on the *Evaluation Worksheet* what the item is and what process(es) should be conducted. Use the Analysis Codes to complete the worksheet.
3. Complete the Post Lab Questions.

Evaluation Worksheet	
Analysis Codes	
Trace = TR	Drugs = DR
Serological/DNA = DNA	Toxicology = TOX
Fingerprints = FP	Questioned = QD
Ballistics/Firearms/Tool marks = FA	

	Item Description	Analysis
Example	12 oz can of soda	DNA, FP
Example	Ransom note on light blue 8.5 by 11 paper	QD, FP
1		
2		
3		
4		
5		
6		
7		
8		
9		
10		

Post Lab Questions

1. For items 1 and 2, justify your analysis selections.
2. Why is it important to maximize the value of evidence?
3. What is the primary goal of drug analysts?
4. Name three different types of biological evidence.

2-3: Fingerprint Pattern Examination

Objectives

- Identify the two main layers of skin.
- Describe the three main fingerprint pattern types.
- Describe various minutiae found in fingerprint patterns.
- Practice identifying the minutiae within a fingerprint.

Materials

- Writing utensil

Concept Overview

In crime scene investigation, fingerprints are some of the most desired types of evidence for recovery. They are considered valuable because they are individualizing, meaning that they can identify an individual as the source of the evidence. The use of fingerprints as a form of identification has occurred for thousands of years. Fingerprints were used by the Chinese as a form of identification on documents in 300 B.C. and as signatures by nobility in India in the 1600s.

The term *fingerprints* has become commonplace with the conception of a fingerprint as the pattern that is present on the tips or first joint of the fingers. However, the individualizing evidence that is on the palms of the hands and soles of the feet results from *friction ridge skin*, which includes fingerprints. Friction ridge skin forms at approximately twelve weeks on the human fetus. This skin has two main layers: dermis and epidermis. The dermis is the innermost layer, while the epidermis is the external layer on which ridges are visible.

Impression evidence derived from friction ridge skin is individualizing because of two important characteristics: uniqueness and permanence. The uniqueness of this type of skin is due to development based on randomness, genetics, and environmental stresses in the womb. To date, no two persons have been found to have the same friction ridge skin, including identical twins who have the same DNA. This skin is also permanent. The friction ridge skin a person is born with will remain relatively unchanged throughout that person's lifetime. Ridge shape and alignment remain constant. Alteration only occurs through injury or damage to the dermal skin layer. Such injury would result in scarring of the epidermis, while damage resulting from certain skin diseases may prevent the formation of friction ridges.

The ridges on the first joint of each finger form one of three distinctive fingerprint patterns. A person may have the same pattern on each finger or have a mixture of two or all three patterns. The most common pattern is the loop (65 percent) (Figure 2.1), followed by the whorl (30 percent) (Figure 2.2), and the least common is the arch (5 percent) (Figure 2.3). The identifying characteristics of a loop are a delta located on one side of the print and a looping feature that enters and exits on the same side of the print. Whorls are

Figure 2.1
Loop

Figure 2.2
Whorl

Figure 2.3
Arch

characterized by a circular pattern in the center of the print and two deltas, one on each side of the center circular pattern. The arch is a pattern characterized by a series of hill shaped ridges of increasing height.

Within friction ridge skin are ridge characteristics known as minutiae or Galton's details (named after Sir Francis Galton). Minutiae consist of ridge endings, short ridges, dots, bifurcations, islands, trifurcations, and spurs (Figures 2.4–2.10).

Examination of fingerprints is through a methodology known as *ACE-V*. The name of the methodology represents the steps in the examination procedure: analysis, comparison, examination, and verification. During the analysis phase, the examiner looks at three levels of detail in a recovered or developed suspect print. Level 1 detail is the fingerprint pattern (loop, whorl, arch). Through level 1 detail, potential donors may be eliminated. For example, a suspect print that is an arch could not have been created by a person who has loop patterns on all fingers. Suspect elimination is possible, but level 1 detail is not enough information to individualize to a specific person. Rather, the examiner must continue on to level 2 detail, which reveals the minutiae of the pattern or friction ridge skin. Analysis is of the ridge characteristics, their location, their relative positions to one another, and explainable dissimilarities. Level 3 details are minute in size and include pores on ridges and the thickness of ridges. In the comparison phase, suspect ink prints are

Ridge Ending

Figure 2.4
Ridge ending

Short Ridge

Figure 2.5
Short ridge

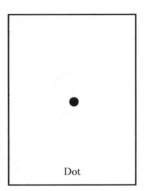

Dot

Figure 2.6
Dot

Bifurcation

Figure 2.7
Bifurcation

Island

Figure 2.8
Island

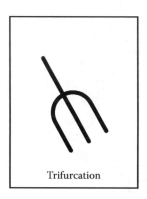

Trifurcation

Figure 2.9
Trifurcation

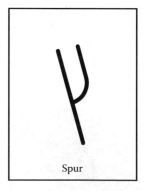

Spur

Figure 2.10
Spur

reviewed for elimination and inclusion for the next phase. In the evaluation phase, the recovered or developed print and suspect inked print(s) are placed side by side and viewed under a loupe or magnification lens. Through this side-by-side analysis, the examiner seeks similarity and dissimilarity. It is in the evaluation phase that an opinion is made as to whether a person is or is not the donor of the print in question. The final phase of the methodology is verification. Another examiner conducts an independent analysis and offers an opinion concerning identification. This is critical as verification can reduce erroneous identifications and prevent self-verification.

Because of the value of friction ridge impression evidence and its potential ramifications for those who are identified as donors of suspect prints, print examination is a critical task. The vast majority of the time, the clarity and quality of recovered and developed prints are not controllable by the processor. This is not so for collected inked prints from suspects. The clarity and quality of these prints is controllable by the collector. Care must be taken to use a minimal amount of ink to prevent filling the furrows of friction ridge skin, which will result in black smudges and no pattern or minutiae reproduction. Using too much pressure during print collection will result in smudging and distortion of prints. Two types of fingerprint impressions will typically be collected: rolled and plain impressions. Rolled impressions are collected by rolling each finger, beginning with the right thumb, nail to nail, recording just below the first finger joint. Plain impressions are collected by simultaneously pressing inked fingers onto a fingerprint card; the thumb is recorded in the same manner, but on a separately designated area of the card.

While ink fingerprinting is still largely used today, computerized alternatives do exist. Live Scan is a computer-based program involving rolling or touching the fingerprint on a glass screen while a computer system records the ridge detail on the finger. The fingerprints are then saved as images and can be used for comparison.

Procedure

1. Create a workstation using butcher paper or similar material to cover the work area surface.
2. Gather the following materials for your workstation:
   - Balloon (uninflated)
   - Ink pad
   - Permanent black marker
3. Slightly inflate your balloon.
4. Using the ink pad, apply ink to one of your fingers. DO NOT overink your finger or the print will smudge.
5. In a down and up motion, place your inked finger on the balloon to apply a print. DO NOT attempt to roll the print.
6. Allow the ink on the balloon to dry.
7. Fully inflate the balloon.
8. Identify the fingerprint pattern on the balloon.
9. Use the marker to circle and label various minutiae in the fingerprint pattern.
10. After completing your print and notating the information in Print 1 of your *Evaluation Worksheet*, trade balloons with a fellow classmate.
11. Examine his or her print and identify, circle, and label minutiae in the print that were not already identified.
12. Notate the information for print 2 of your *Evaluation Worksheet*.
13. Draw a replication of your plain fingerprint in the sketch canvas provided.
14. Complete Post Lab Questions.

Evaluation Worksheet

Print 1:

What is the fingerprint pattern?   Loop   Whorl   Arch

Notate the number of each type of minutiae in the print which is on the balloon:

Bifurcation: _____

Dot: _____

Ending Ridge: _____

Island: _____

Trifurcation: _____

Short Ridge: _____

Spur: _____

Print 2:

What is the fingerprint pattern?   Loop   Whorl   Arch

Notate the number of each type of minutiae in the print which is on the balloon:

Bifurcation: _____

Dot: _____

Ending Ridge: _____

Island: _____

Trifurcation: _____

Short Ridge: _____

Spur: _____

Sketch Canvas

Post Lab Questions

1. Was it difficult to identify the minutiae in your print? Why or why not?
2. How many different minutiae were identified in your print?
3. Were there any similarities and/or differences between prints 1 and 2? If so, describe.
4. What does ACE-V stand for?
5. Name the three basic fingerprint patterns.
6. What does level 3 detail of the analysis phase encompass?

2-4: False Positive Exercise

Objectives

- Understand the concept of positive and negative controls.
- Describe a false positive.
- Utilize a chemical process to understand false positives.

Materials

- Writing utensil
- Timing device

Concept Overview

When conducting chemical tests it is important to confirm whether the process is working correctly or not. Before using the chemicals on any evidentiary items, a positive and negative control should be used. A positive control is conducted with a sample that is known, such as blood from an individual. Using the chemical test on this sample should always yield a positive result. The failure to produce a positive result could be due to the chemical's exhausted shelf life or result if a chemical was not prepared or stored properly. A positive control ensures the reagents used in the test are working properly and they are safe to use on evidentiary samples. A negative control should also be used when the sample is on a medium, for example, when blood drops are found on dark dyed blue jeans. A piece of the dark dyed jeans should be tested with no blood to ensure the dyes used in the material do not yield a positive result. The results of a negative control should always be negative. If a negative control is not used and the dark dyed jeans have a property that reacts with the chemical, a false positive may result. A false positive occurs when the chemical test reacts to a sample that is not the stain being tested. This could cause significant investigative issues and lead to wrongful prosecution and incarceration.

Procedure

1. Create a workstation using butcher paper or similar material to cover the work area surface.
2. Gather the following materials for your workstation
   - Writing utensil
   - Timing device
   - Hemastix

3. Using the yellow tip end of the Hemastix, touch the tip (pad) of the stick to the red substance provided.
4. Observe the pad for a maximum of five minutes.
5. Record the color change and the reaction time (time it took for the pad to turn colors).
6. Repeat this process for the same stain before moving forward. (Each stain should be tested twice to show concordance with the first result.)
7. Record all information in the *Data Worksheet*.
8. Once all samples have been tested, smell each stain and record what *you* believe the stain to be. Please note: Smelling stains should only be done in the context of an exercise that has been designed for smelling. This should *NEVER* be done at a crime scene or during laboratory work.
9. Complete the Post Lab Questions.

Data Worksheet

Stain	Time	Color
1		
2		
3		
4		

SMELL IDENTIFICATION OF SAMPLES:

1. _____
2. _____
3. _____
4. _____

Post Lab Questions

1. Did any of the samples provided create a false positive?
2. How many samples did you correctly identify by smell?
3. What is a positive control?
4. Why are negative controls important?

2-5: Mechanical Fit through Evidence Reconstruction

Objectives

- Describe mechanical fit.
- Examine pieces of torn evidence for reconstruction of evidence and individualization through mechanical fit.

Materials

- Clean work area
- Glue or tape
- Writing utensil

Concept Overview

Mechanical fit, also known as a fracture match, is a unique form of evidence. When damaged or broken pieces of an object are in a scene, they may be reconstructed. These pieces should be carefully collected to prevent further breakage and preserved in their original form. When the item of origin is located, the pieces may be examined and pieced back to the original object. This is known as mechanical fit or fracture matching. This is much like putting a puzzle together. Since the breaking action creates randomly sized and shaped pieces, the pieces matched back to the item of origin can be viewed as individualizing evidence.

Procedure

1. Examine the provided evidentiary pieces.
2. Lay the pieces out onto the workbook *Reconstruction Canvas* and glue pieces together to visually demonstrate mechanical fit.
3. Complete the Post Lab Questions.

Reconstruction Canvas

Post Lab Questions

1. What is mechanical fit?
2. Was using mechanical fit successful for both of the above items? Explain.
3. Describe each of the reconstructed evidentiary items.
4. How could mechanical fit be beneficial to an investigation?
5. Give an example of an item, other than paper, that could yield mechanical fit.

Works Cited

Gardner, Ross M. *Practical Crime Scene Processing and Investigation.* Boca Raton, FL: CRC Press, 2005.

Houck, Max M., and Jay A. Siegel. *Fundamentals of Forensic Science.* San Diego, CA: Academic Press, 2009.

James, Stuart H., and Jon J. Nordby. *Forensic Science: An Introduction to Scientific and Investigative Techniques.* 3rd ed. Boca Raton, FL: CRC Press, 2009.

3

Actions of the Initial Responding Officer

Key Terms

Initial responding officer
Primary focal points
Secondary scenes
Natural entry and exit points

Learning Outcomes

1. Understand the importance of being the first responding officer.

2. Identify primary focal points and natural entry and exit points.

3. Recognize the value associated with secondary scenes.

3-1: Creating a Crime Scene Control Log

Objectives

- Understand the importance of crime scene security.
- Understand the importance of crime scene integrity.
- Practice creating a formal crime scene control log.

Materials

- Paper
- Writing utensil
- Alternate: Computer/word processing software

Concept Overview

The initial responding officer is a key player in keeping and maintaining the crime scene until all other personnel arrive on scene. Their main objectives should be to:

1. Document the provided information.
2. Not become a casualty.
3. Provide for emergency care.
4. Secure and control the scene, including all persons within it.
5. Release the scene to the appropriate authorities. (Usually this will be the investigating detective and/or crime scene personnel.)

Documenting the initial information is an important step in verifying information relayed from dispatch and taking down basic scene information. This can include but is not limited to:

1. Case number.
2. Address of the incident.
3. Type of crime/call.
4. Arrival/departure times.
5. Complainant/victim/eye witnesses and/or suspects information.
6. Personnel entering and leaving the scene and the reason they are there.

Confirming and documenting this information allows the initial responding officer to have a solid foundation when moving forward in the scene.

Officer safety is an important key in any investigation. Many times officers rush into a scene in their desire to improve the situation and do not consider the threats or dangers that could lie just around the corner. When gauging officer safety, three specific areas should be considered:

1. Is the crime still in progress and are there suspects on scene?
2. Are there natural hazards present that can inhibit or harm the first responder?
3. Are there man-made hazards present that can endanger first responders?

Once these areas have been addressed, officers can proceed more cautiously and effectively into a scene.

Emergency care is generally administered by emergency medical services (EMS) personnel. In crimes involving an injury or death, an additional factor to consider is controlling the lifesaving activities and medical personnel who respond. While police agencies mandate evidence preservation, *lifesaving always takes priority over evidence preservation.* If the initial responding officer arrives before EMS, the officer must take steps to aid the victim. If the officer is not participating in the lifesaving actions, the responding officer can direct medical personnel and others entering the scene in order to preserve the scene as best as possible.

Once the scene is safe and lifesaving activities under way or completed, the initial responding officer must try to secure and control the crime scene. Every crime scene is different, and in deciding on where to establish the perimeter, several things should be considered:

1. Is there a primary focal point?
2. Is there a natural entry or exit point?
3. Is there a secondary scene? Could it be possible a secondary scene exists?

The primary focal point is the easiest to detect. This is the area where an officer will naturally gravitate toward upon arrival at the scene. Generally these areas include a body laying on the floor in the middle of a room or, in the case of a burglary, a ransacked living room. The natural entry or exit points are also of particular interest in a crime scene. Perpetrators must enter and leave a scene in some manner such as entering by breaking in and exiting by driving away. Oftentimes these areas are rich in evidentiary value and should be noted. Examples of possible evidence include blood evidence, fingerprint impressions, trace evidence, and tire or footwear impressions. By linking the natural focal point with the entry and exit points, the officer can isolate the areas included in the primary scene.

A potentially significant issue is to overlook secondary scenes. Such areas may include staging areas, areas where goods were loaded up to be used in the commission of the crime, or areas where items were deposited after the crime took place. These areas are often located in close proximity to the scene and/or along avenues of entry or exit.

Eventually the investigating detective and/or crime scene personnel will arrive to assume responsibility of the scene. The releasing of the scene could take minutes or it could take hours. This is an opportune time for the initial responding officer to make notes regarding the scene and to note observations and his or her actions upon arrival at the scene. It is imperative that the initial responding officer be debriefed by the investigative personnel at the scene before responding to his or her next call or scene.

Procedure

1. Examine the *Data Table* of provided category terms and create a template for a crime scene control log.
2. When satisfied with the template, create a formal log.
3. Complete the Post Lab Questions.

The data table contains the category terms to be used in creating a crime scene control log template and formal document.

Data Table

Date	Time Out	Form Creator
Location Address	Reason at Scene (additional personnel)	Name/Unit/Agency
Case Number	Time In	Offense

Post Lab Questions

1. What is the purpose of a crime scene log?
2. What items should be included in the log?
3. Why is debriefing important?
4. Define and give an example of a primary focal point.
5. Which area, primary focal point or natural entry and exit point, is the most important to preserve? Why?

Works Cited

Gardner, Ross M. *Practical Crime Scene Processing and Investigation.* Boca Raton, FL: CRC Press, 2005.

Chapter 4

Processing Methodology

Key Terms

Assessing
Observing
Documenting
Searching
Collecting
Processing/Analyzing
"Going back"

Learning Outcomes

1. Identify the six basic activities related to crime scene processing.
2. Identify, in order, the sequence of each activity.
3. Understand the process of "going back."
4. Recognize the eight-step descriptive set.

4-1: Utilizing a Descriptive Set in Evidence Documentation

Objectives

- Describe the basic activities upon discovering evidentiary items.
- Describe the eight-step descriptive set used to document evidence.
- Practice using the eight-step descriptive set to demonstrate evidence.

Materials

- Writing utensil

Concept Overview

Crime scene processing is accomplished through the following basic activities: assessing, observing, documenting, searching, collecting, and processing/analyzing.

Assessing begins the task of processing and defines which procedures will be used. This is a continuous process as the crime scene is processed. It is important for crime scene personnel to assess the scene and adjust the processing plan when necessary.

Observing involves evaluating and mentally registering the condition of the scene and items located within it. It is important to remember when observing that this does not always mean moving through the scene in an intrusive manner. Many times crime scene personnel must consciously act only to observe from a single point and not move through the scene and possibly disturb or damage valuable physical evidence.

Documenting is a critical component in crime scene processing. It includes numerous activities including written documentation of the crime scene personnel's observations, photographing and videotaping the scene and its evidence, and the creation of crime scene sketches. These activities range from nonintrusive (taking overall photographs) to very intrusive (taking measurements for a crime scene sketch). It is important to make sure the initial documentation of the scene captures the scene in situ, or as is, before any significant scene alterations occur. When documenting the scene, it is important to detail each item located at the scene. An eight-step descriptive set may be used to complete this task. The eight steps include:

1. Quantity
2. Item
3. Color
4. Type of Construction
5. Approximate size
6. Identifying features
7. Condition
8. Location

Searching the scene ranges from visually examining the scene to moving items within the crime scene to observe their surfaces. Because of the intrusive nature of this task, it is important that all initial documentation be completed before continuing with a more intrusive and disruptive search.

Collecting is the physical collection of items within the crime scene. Such items can include trace evidence, blood evidence, impression evidence, or objects or items in the scene that contain these types of evidence. Collection may also be of structural objects such as pieces of flooring and walls that contain some or all of the aforementioned evidence. It must be remembered that once an item is removed from the scene, the scene is forever altered.

Processing the scene involves the use of powders or chemicals in order to develop, enhance, or make visible items of evidence. Black powder, magnetic powder, and superglue fuming are all examples of techniques that can be used to develop latent prints. In regards to potential blood evidence, presumptive tests such as phenolphthalein or tetramethylbenzidine (TMB) may be employed as a screening process prior to utilizing blood development and enhancement chemicals such as amido black and luminol. In some situations, it may be necessary to use more than one development technique. It is the responsibility of the crime scene technician to consider which methods can and will be used in order to determine the sequence in which they need to be employed. This knowledge is the result of training and experience. Ultimately, each item of evidence will be submitted for some form of analysis, and each piece will be used to determine a sequence of events that took place within the scene.

"Going back" is an integral part of crime scene processing and is a common and necessary occurrence. The farther one progresses into the processing of a scene, the more likely it is that personnel will encounter items that were not previously observed or considered to have probative value. As a result, new items of evidence are routinely discovered. When this occurs, the investigator or technician must cease his or her current step and return to an earlier one, such as documentation, in order to deal with the newly discovered evidence. This process will occur throughout the entire scene processing event. It will end when no more evidence or potential evidence is observed.

Now that the basic processing activities have been identified, the questions an investigator may ask are: How do I apply them to a scene? Is there a particular order or sequence in which these activities should be conducted? There is no one correct way to process a scene. There is no single sequential template that can be used to investigate and process every scene. This is because all scenes have unique circumstances and characteristics. Variation will occur in the following:

- location (indoors vs. outdoors)
- environmental characteristics
  - outdoors: rain, wind, extreme temperatures
  - indoors: no ventilation, no electricity
- condition of decedent
  - advanced decomposition
  - dismemberment
  - fire damage
- evidence processing/collection (type and extent)
  - trace evidence
  - fingerprint/friction ridge processing
  - blood evidence
  - chemical processing/enhancement
- impression casting

Even though such variation will always be encountered, it is imperative that investigators and technicians use some type of methodology in their investigations. A methodology is the procedure by which one conducts an activity. Use of a methodology in scene investigation and processing will necessarily cause the investigative event to be more focused and thereby more efficient. Focus and efficiency will increase the quality of every aspect of an investigation. This is certainly not to say that one is locked into the sequence outlined in a given methodology. On the contrary, investigators must be flexible and adaptable as scene investigations are fluid and dynamic. Typically, there is movement among the steps or processes within a methodology. An investigative methodology developed by the U.S. Army Criminal Investigation Command is offered as an example:

Step 1: Initial Notification—This information concerns who contacted the investigator, when contact was made, the type of scene reported, and who made the report.

Step 2: Coordination, Assessment, and Team Call-Out—This step involves confirming the jurisdiction of the scene, assessment of the scene after arrival, and determining whether additional investigative personnel will be needed for the scene investigation.

Step 3: Conduct Initial Observations—The investigator conducts an initial scan of the scene. Fragile evidence observed is immediately collected to prevent loss. Otherwise, focal points or central theme items such as a decedent or weapon are visually searched for to gain an overall impression of the scene.

Step 4: Deal with the Deceased—An inquest or investigation by a medical examiner or justice of the peace should be conducted in all instances of questioned death. An investigator must find out the specific actions carried out during such inquests and document them. Movement of the decedent, inadvertent repositioning of the decedent or decedent's clothing can affect theories generated concerning actions within the scene. This same information must be obtained from emergency service personnel if attempted aid was administered.

Step 5: Photograph the Scene—The scene is documented with video and photography. Photographs should be of three ranges: overall, medium range or evidence establishing, and closeup.

Step 6: Document Overall Observations—The eight-step descriptive set, listed previously, is used to obtain detailed information of the scene and its evidence. At this point, the observation is done visually. Objects or items of the scene are not touched or moved as the evidence within the scene has not been plotted and sketched yet.

Step 7: Sketch the Scene—A rough or preliminary sketch is created to document the dimensions of the rooms and furniture of the scene. Evidence is also plotted or fixed within the scene using measurements obtained through one of several mapping methods. Accurate measurements at times requires the movement of items within the scene. Thus, sketching is a task conducted after photography.

Step 8: Conduct a First Recheck—The scene is observed visually for items that may have been missed up to this point in the investigation.

Step 9: Release the Body—Prior to movement of the decedent for transport, thorough observation and visual examination must be conducted for fragile evidence or evidence that may be altered during transport. Such evidence should be documented and collected.

Step 10: Collect Items of Evidence—Items identified as evidence are moved and evaluated for other types of evidence such as trace evidence or blood evidence. If found, the evidence is photographed and collected for analysis. All items should be collected and properly packaged.

Step 11: Conduct a Second Recheck of the Scene—Now that all identified evidence has been collected, the investigator can begin processing for fingerprints, utilizing an alternate light source (ALS) to search for biological fluids, and items may be moved and turned over in search of additional physical evidence.

Step 12: Conduct a Third Recheck of the Scene—This involves confirming that no area of the scene has been overlooked in the searching process. More complex techniques such as chemical enhancement and trajectory analysis are conducted.

Step 13: Check beyond the Scene—The scene perimeter and outlying areas are rechecked to confirm that no evidence has been overlooked.

Step 14: Conduct an On-Scene Debriefing of the Investigative Team—Prior to releasing the scene, team members ensure that all documentation has been collected and any investigative questions concerning the scene have been answered, if possible.

Step 15: Release or Secure the Scene—The scene is to be released to the appropriate person, and once released, the scene cannot be captured again without a warrant or consent.

Step 16: Process and Package Evidence—In a controlled environment, the investigator or technician ensures that all evidence is properly packaged for preservation.

Step 17: Conduct a Formal Debriefing—Case agents review the investigation and consider working theories based on the information obtained.

This seventeen-step methodology is quite extensive and is typically utilized in its entirety when major crime scene investigations, such as homicide, are conducted. Nonetheless, any crime scene may be investigated by employing this methodology. It may be necessary, however, to exclude unnecessary steps.

Procedure

1. Examine the evidentiary items provided by the instructor.

2. In the *Data Worksheet* document each item using the eight-step descriptive set.

3. Complete the Post Lab Questions.

Data Worksheet

Item	
Descriptive set	
Quantity	
Item	
Color	
Type of construction	
Approximate size	
Identifying features	
Condition	
Location	

Item	
Descriptive set	
Quantity	
Item	
Color	
Type of construction	
Approximate size	
Identifying features	
Condition	
Location	

Data Worksheet

Item	
Descriptive set	
Quantity	
Item	
Color	
Type of construction	
Approximate size	
Identifying features	
Condition	
Location	

Item	
Descriptive set	
Quantity	
Item	
Color	
Type of construction	
Approximate size	
Identifying features	
Condition	
Location	

Data Worksheet

Item	
Descriptive set	
Quantity	
Item	
Color	
Type of construction	
Approximate size	
Identifying features	
Condition	
Location	

Item	
Descriptive set	
Quantity	
Item	
Color	
Type of construction	
Approximate size	
Identifying features	
Condition	
Location	

Post Lab Questions

1. What are the six basic steps associated with crime scene processing?
2. What eight elements are associated with the descriptive set?
3. What is the purpose of observing?
4. Do you always have to walk through a crime scene to observe?
5. Give an example of "going back" at a scene.
6. Why is important to make sure you have completed initial documentation before moving forward?
7. If an item at the scene is "bumped," unintentionally moved, can one just put it back? Why or why not?

Works Cited

Gardner, Ross M. *Practical Crime Scene Processing and Investigation.* Boca Raton, FL: CRC Press, 2005.

Chapter **5**

Assessing the Scene

Key Terms

Biohazard
Circle or spiral search
Grid search
Scene security
Strip and line search
Zone search
Team approach: area
Team approach: function

Learning Outcomes

1. Understand each of the crime scene searching techniques.
2. Define area and function team approaches.
3. Recognize common biohazards.

5-1:   Establishing Crime Scene Perimeters

Objectives

- Understand the purpose of crime scene perimeters.
- Describe the function of the inner scene perimeter and outer scene perimeter.
- Examine crime scene figures and practice establishing crime scene perimeters.

Materials

- Writing utensil

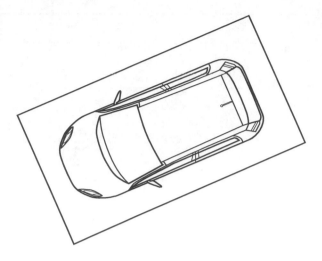

Figure 5.1
Initial scene perimeter

Concept Overview

The basic goal of scene processing is to collect as much evidence as possible in the best condition possible. The best way to preserve the integrity of the evidence is to produce a multilevel isolation.

The initial crime scene perimeter is likely to consist of a single barrier established by the initial responding officer (Figure 5.1). Its placement is based on observations at the scene involving the natural focal point and entry and exit points. The primary focal point is the area that an officer will naturally gravitate toward upon scene arrival such as the location of a decent or a weapon. The natural entry or exit points are rich in evidentiary value and should also be protected. Such areas can contain trace evidence, impression evidence, or blood evidence of the suspect(s). By linking the natural focal point with the entry and exit points, the officer has isolated areas of evidentiary value for the investigator. Crime scene barriers are put in place using a variety of methods. Crime scene tape, law enforcement personnel or vehicles, and natural boundary lines such as a river or stream or heavily wooded area are all means of providing a barrier for a crime scene.

Even though the initial responding officer has established an initial perimeter to protect the scene, crime scene personnel and investigators must conduct an independent evaluation of the entire scene. A decision must be made to either maintain the established initial perimeter or create a larger or smaller inner barrier (Figure 5.2).

After establishing the inner perimeter, another assessment should be made to determine whether the establishment of an outer perimeter is warranted. One factor affecting this decision concern physical scene characteristics. For example, is the scene in a secluded, rural area or in a highly populated urban area? The number of personnel on location is also a factor. An outer perimeter may be necessary to isolate the scene and the investigators working in it. The second barrier should be far enough away to control onlookers and the media while giving enough room between the initial and secondary barriers for officers and crime scene personnel to gather. This "buffer zone" should be used as a working area. It also provides a physical buffer between the actual scene and unauthorized individuals.

Secondary scenes should also be considered when assessing the crime scene for security issues. Before or after the commission of the crime, staging areas or areas where goods may have been loaded, stored, or

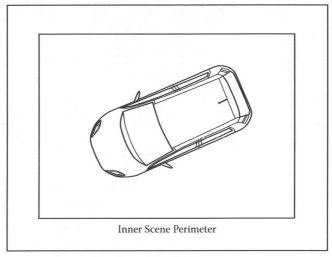

Inner Scene Perimeter

Outer Scene Perimeter

Figure 5.2
Established inner and outer perimeters

discarded could contain evidence that is pertinent to the case. It is important for officers and crime scene personnel alike to consider secondary scenes when establishing crime scene barriers.

In any attempt to search or process a crime scene, all personnel involved need to be conscious of biohazard risks that may be present. Hazards come in a variety of forms. Structural hazards may be found in fire or explosion scenes. Chemical or inhalation hazards from fire scenes or natural gas leaks may also be present. Biological biohazards are often the products of the crime itself and are seen in the form of blood, fecal matter, urine, vomit, dirty needles or syringes, and so forth. These hazards, if precautions are not taken, could lead to exposure to HIV, hepatitis A, B, or C, or ultimately illness and possibly death. It is important to make sure all personal protective equipment (PPE) is in place, including, but not limited to, masks or breathing apparatus, gloves, booties, Tyvek suits, and eye protection.

Procedure

1. Examine the provided crime scene diagrams.
2. For each figure, draw an inner perimeter based on:
   • primary focal points
   • natural entry and exit points
   • secondary scenes
   Identify and describe each of these elements in the *Data Worksheets*.
3. For each figure, draw an outer perimeter if necessary and indicate on the diagram the locations of the following:
   • crime scene investigators
   • general law enforcement personnel
   • administration staff
   • media
   • onlookers
4. Complete the Post Lab Questions.

Data Worksheet

In the data worksheet below, indicate the specific characteristics present in the scene which affected the creation of the inner and/or outer perimeter. This information should support the location and boundaries of the inner and/or outer perimeter.

Scene Scope	Scene Characteristic(s)
Primary focal points	
Natural entry and exit points	
Secondary scenes	

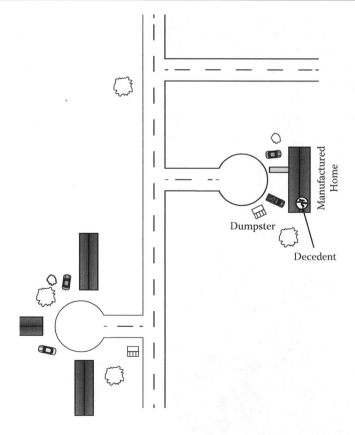

Figure 5.3
Scene Diagram

Data Worksheet

Scene Scope	Scene Characteristic(s)
Primary focal points	
Natural entry and exit points	
Secondary scenes	

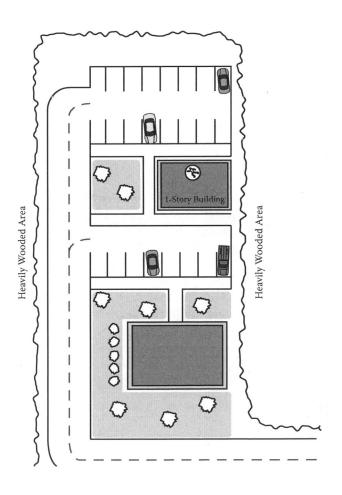

Figure 5.4
Scene Diagram

Data Worksheet

Scene Scope	Scene Characteristic(s)
Primary focal points	
Natural entry and exit points	
Secondary scenes	

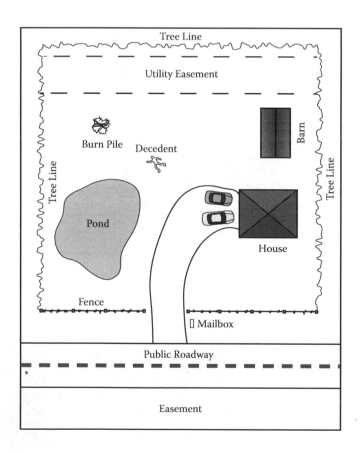

Figure 5.5
Scene Diagram

Post Lab Questions

1. What is the purpose of an initial crime scene barrier? Who is generally responsible for putting up this barrier?
2. Why is a secondary barrier important?
3. When looking at the diagrams, was it easy or difficult to determine where to draw the crime scene barriers? Why or why not?
4. Who is generally located in the buffer zone between the two crime scene barriers?
5. What are some disadvantages of using a natural barrier?

5-2: Conducting Crime Scene Searches

Objectives

- Describe the five basic crime scene search patterns.
- Practice conducting crime scene searches.

Materials

- Writing utensil

Concept Overview

Searching of the scene is required to locate evidence that is present. The specific method chosen will vary based on the team composition and the location or area of the scene. It is important to be methodical and systematic when searching the scene. Methodical refers to the order or systematic behavior related to searching the scene. Systematic refers to being purposefully regular, which helps to eliminate overlooking key evidentiary items. The combination of being methodical and systematic ensures the searcher or searchers have thoroughly covered the area to the best of their ability. Several things are taken into consideration when determining which search method to use:

1. Nature of the ground being covered
2. Lighting conditions
3. On-scene environmental conditions
4. Size of the item being searched for

Scene searches may also be conducted by a single searcher or multiple searchers depending on the area that needs to be searched. When a team is required, it is important to select a specific approach to utilize, either by area or function. The area approach is where a single team handles all activities associated with processing the scene. The function approach is when a team leader designates different groups of people to do different activities at the scene. Whether by area or by function, it is of vital importance to establish a plan for processing the scene.

Although there are many different types of search methods, this activity will concentrate on four:

1. Circle or spiral search
2. Strip or line search
3. Grid search
4. Zone search

A circle or spiral search is a useful method when searching interior scenes. The searcher begins from the outside perimeter, then moving in a circular motion, works inward toward the middle of the scene making a spiral pattern. This technique can also be conducted in the reverse, beginning at the interior of the scene and working one's way toward the perimeter in a spiral pattern. Whether moving inward or outward, it is important to keep a constant pace.

The strip or line search is effective when searching a large exterior area. Examples include large open parking lots and yards. The area is divided into strips. In a strip search a single searcher begins on an outer strip and moves down the line. Once at the end of the line, the searcher reverses direction and searches the adjacent line until the whole scene has been searched. Using the same "strip" technique, a line search is a variation of the strip search using multiple searchers. The area is again divided into strips; however, a line of searchers moves over the area simultaneously, covering the entire area at once.

The grid search is another effective search technique that is a variation of the line search. Instead of limiting the search to strips orientated in a single direction, the grid search allows searchers to conduct the search again using strips at a right angle to the original lines. In effect, the search covers all four compass directions thus allowing a second look for the searcher and ensuring a more effective search.

The zone search is used in two variations. The first variation deals with very small confined spaces that are not easily searched by any other method. An example of this would be a vehicle. A vehicle could be easily divided into zones, allowing the searcher to look at each defined area before moving forward. The second variation involves large scenes that need to be broken down, or subdivided, into smaller areas or zones to be searched effectively. This allows searchers to break down and prioritize areas. Breaking down larger areas also lends itself to incorporating a line or strip, grid, or spiral or circle search in each designated zone, allowing for a maximum search effort.

When searching for evidentiary items, a number of methods may be used to mark evidentiary items found. Flags or evidence placards affixed with numbers or letters are often the most commonly encountered at a scene.

Procedure

1. Examine the characteristics of the crime scene to determine which search method to employ.
2. In the *Data Worksheet*, describe the scene characteristics that support the chosen search method.
3. Upon discovering evidentiary items, signify them with a placard or flag.
4. Determine an alternative search method should your first choice not be available. Defend your choice of the chosen alternative method.
5. Complete the *Data Worksheet*.
6. Complete the Post Lab Questions.

Data Worksheet

	Search Method	Characteristics of Scene
Primary Search Method		
Alternative Search Method		
Defend the choice of the alternative search method.		

	Search Method	Characteristics of Scene
Primary Search Method		
Alternative Search Method		
Defend the choice of the alternative search method.		

Post Lab Questions

1. When is a spiral or circle search used?
2. How many evidentiary items were located at the scene? Describe each.
3. Describe the similarities and differences between the strip and line searches.
4. Describe the two variations of a zone search. Give an example of each.
5. Name and describe the two team approaches.

Works Cited

Gardner, Ross M. *Practical Crime Scene Processing and Investigation.* Boca Raton, FL: CRC Press, 2005.

Chapter 6

Crime Scene Photography

Key Terms

Overall photographs
Midrange photographs
Evidence closeup photographs
Wide-angle lens
Roadmapping
Scale
Photo placard
Photography log
Fragile evidence
Shutter speed
Focal length
Tripod
Fill-flash
Overexposure
Oblique lighting
Diffuser
Bounce lighting
F/stop
Depth of field
Single lens reflex (SLR) camera
Painting with light
Bulb setting

Learning Outcomes

- Understand the modes associated with a camera: program, aperture priority, shutter priority, and manual mode.
- Recognize the importance of depth of field.
- Understand the importance of range photographs for comprehensive scene photography.

6-1: Photography in Manual Mode

Objectives

- Describe the three elements that determine a proper photographic exposure in the manual mode.
- Understand the exposure level scale as a function of proper image capture in the manual mode.
- Practice image capture in manual mode.

Materials

- Digital camera
- Writing utensil

Concept Overview

For the documentation of crime scenes, a digital single lens reflex (SLR) camera is the appropriate type of camera to use versus a digital point and shoot. An SLR camera contains mirrors and prisms that allow the photographer to see the image in the viewfinder as the lens captures the image. The lens is removable from the body of the camera, which makes the digital SLR camera very versatile. For example, an investigator may require the use of lenses with varying focal lengths or, when focused on infinity, the distance between the film plane and the optical center of the lens. For a 35-mm digital SLR camera, a normal lens is 50 mm, a wide angle lens is less than 50 mm, and a telephoto lens is greater than 50 mm; a macro lens captures subjects 1:1 or life size. Further, this type of camera has the ability to capture images in several types of modes: program, aperture priority, shutter priority, and manual mode. The multiple modes of the camera allow the photographer to capture images based on the characteristics of the subject matter. Moreover, a photographer is capable of maximizing the depth of field of evidentiary items with a digital SLR camera. Depth of field is the zone of focus in a variable range in front of and to the rear of the subject matter. The vast majority of the time the goal of the crime scene photographer is to maximize the depth of field when capturing images. In contrast, digital point and shoot cameras are not capable of the desired versatility required to accurately and properly document crime scenes.

To achieve a proper photographic exposure, three camera elements are manipulated: f/stop, shutter speed, and film speed (sensor sensitivity). The films used in film cameras have various speeds expressed as ISO (International Organization for Standardization) numbers. Film speed relates to its sensitivity to light. Common film speeds are ISO50, ISO100, ISO200, ISO400, ISO800, ISO1600. The lower the ISO number, the less sensitive the film is to light or less light is needed to capture an image.

Digital cameras do not use film. Instead, they contain digital sensors that can be adjusted by the user. The ISO numbers have been maintained within the digital camera and refer to light sensitivity for the digital sensors. As a rule of thumb, cameras should be set to ISO400 when indoors and ISO100 when outdoors on a bright, sunny day.

F/stops or f-numbers (also referred to as aperture) relate to the size of the opening of the lens when capturing an image. The f/stop is directly related to the amount of light that is allowed to enter into the lens during capture. The lower the f/stop number, the greater the size of the lens opening and thus more light is allowed to enter the lens. The larger the f/stop number, the smaller the size of the lens opening and thus less light is allowed to enter the lens. This, at first, may seem counterintuitive until one understands that the f/stop is a *fraction of the focal length of the lens being used*. Thus, regardless of the lens used, 1/22 of a number is always smaller than 1/8 of a number (Figure 6.1).

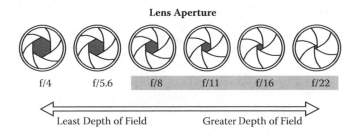

Figure 6.1
Lens aperture

When first learning to manipulate f/stops, captured images may be overexposed or contain more light than is normal and desired; images may also be underexposed or contain less light than is normal or desired.

Shutter speed relates to the amount of time the lens is allowed to remain open during the capture of an image; it is usually expressed in fractions of a second. It is this camera variable that affects motion control. Thus, when setting the proper shutter speed for the characteristics of the subject matter, the subject will appear stationary, free of motion and blur. Shutter speed also compensates for motion of the camera as well as motion of the photographer. As a rule of thumb, setting a camera's shutter speed to 1/60 of a second will prevent image blur due to camera movement, also known as camera shake. If shutter speeds less than 1/60 of a second are used, a tripod will be necessary. A tripod is a piece of stabilization equipment or platform on which a camera is attached. When taking photographs with a tripod, it is important to prevent the introduction of movement. Thus, a shutter release cable or the camera's internal timer is used for image capture rather than physically touching the camera during capture. Shutter speed is a powerful photographic tool as it can freeze the motion of a variety of activities using high shutter speeds such as walking, talking, jogging, slow moving vehicles, and fast moving vehicles. In contrast, the bulb (B) setting may be used to keep the lens open for an amount of time to be determined by the photographer. This time may vary from 30 seconds to 3 minutes to 3 hours. It is in the B setting that a lighting technique known as *painting with light* is conducted. Through this technique, a large dimly lit area may be photographed by adding light from a camera flash or flashlight. When first learning to manipulate shutter speeds, captured images may be overexposed or underexposed. Practice will improve the ability to use this variable.

The investigator's goal is to learn how to properly manipulate f/stop and shutter speed variables for image capture. When this is accomplished, both may be manipulated to obtain optimal images in the camera's manual mode. With so many potential combinations between f/stop and shutter speed and ISO, it may be difficult to choose a starting point. Some guidelines may assist.

1. When indoors, set the camera to ISO400; when outdoors on a bright, sunny day, set the camera to ISO100.
2. Setting the shutter speed to 1/60 will allow the camera to be hand held and not require stabilization by a tripod.

With the ISO and shutter speed tentatively selected, this leaves the f/stop. F/stop is one of the variables that directly affects the depth of field that will result in the captured image. Recall that in crime scene photography, with very few exceptions, depth of field (DOF) should be maximized, and this is the purpose for manipulating f/stop and not using the program (automatic) mode of the camera. In program mode, the camera makes the setting decisions, and the f/stop that results is always the lowest f/stop number possible. These low f/stop numbers result in shallow DOF, the opposite of the DOF desired for crime scene photographs. This leads to a guideline for f/stops.

3. To maximize DOF, set the camera to one of the following: f/8, f/11, f/16, f/22.

An exception to guideline 3 is the desire to capture an object and obscure (blur) the background. To achieve an image such as this, the f/stop would be set to the lowest number possible. Occasions when an investigator or technician may wish to do this is when the only focus of the captured image is an evidentiary item,

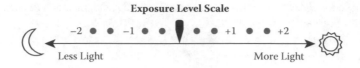

Figure 6.2
Exposure level scale

such as a fired cartridge case or broken piece of glass. To prevent the viewer from being distracted by the background upon which the evidence is lying or to prevent the item from being lost among its background, the f/stop may be set very low so that only the desired object is in focus while everything else within the camera's frame is blurred.

Following these three guidelines, a starting point for a proper exposure has been set. This does not guarantee a proper exposure, however. The photographer uses the exposure level scale visible in the camera viewfinder (and on the liquid crystal display [LCD] screens of some cameras) to determine whether there must be continued manipulation of the f/stop or shutter speed (Figure 6.2).

When the exposure level mark is in the center of the scale, as depicted in Figure 6.2, the camera is indicating a properly metered exposure. Moving the mark to the left or right of center will either add or decrease the brightness of the captured image. The best practice when taking important photographs is to take at least three photographs. One marked in the center of the scale, one marked adding a stop of light (+1), and one marked removing a stop of light (−1). This process of multiple photographs of the same subject with different values of light is called *bracketing*. It must be stated that a camera is a mechanical device and fallible. Photographers will find that at times a properly metered exposure, as indicated by the camera's exposure level scale, will be either overexposed or underexposed.

An important piece of photographic equipment is an off-camera flash. Digital SLR cameras have built-in popup flashes, but these are limiting due to their light output. Off-camera flashes have much more power than popup flashes and are much more versatile. They can be positioned in a variety of angles. When they are angled so that the flash bounces off of ceilings or walls, this is known as the bounce lighting technique. This technique, through the bouncing of light from surfaces, will allow softer light to fall on the subject rather than using harsh, direct lighting. Another technique for softening light falling on a subject is the use of a diffuser. A diffuser is a piece of equipment, usually a piece of plastic that covers the flash to diffuse the harshness of the emitted light. The use of a remote flash cord also enhances the versatility of the off-camera flash. This cord connects to the camera's hot-shoe (a fitting on a camera containing an electrical contact) and to the off-camera flash. In this configuration, the photographer holds the camera in one hand while holding the flash in the other. The flash can then be directed to any location in which light is needed. For example, oblique lighting or side lighting, which is accomplished by holding the flash at 45 degrees or less, is a photographic lighting technique that would not be possible if the flash could not be manipulated away from the camera body. Oblique lighting is very useful when photographing impression evidence such as footwear, tool marks, and bite marks. Another valuable flash technique is known as fill-flash. This technique is employed when there are shadowed areas in the composition. The flash is positioned so that the emitted light falls onto the shadowed area to illuminate it.

Procedure: F/stop

1. Set digital camera to manual setting; all photographs will be taken in this setting.
2. Set the camera to ISO100 if photographing outdoors; set the camera to ISO400 if photographing indoors.
3. Set the camera's shutter speed to at least 1/30 or 1/60 to allow hand holding of the camera without camera shake or use of a tripod.

4. Set the camera's f/stop to its lowest number (f/4, f/5.6, f/8) and take a photograph of a subject. Record the settings used to capture the image in the provided photography log.

5. Maintain all camera settings except the f/stop and change it to the highest number (f/16, f/22, f/32) and take a photograph of the same subject as in step 4. Record the camera settings in the photography log.

6. Compare the two images to visualize the function of f/stops.

7. Maintain the camera settings and manipulate only the f/stop. Photograph the same subject using the full range of f/stops available for your camera. Record the settings of each photograph. Review your photographs.

8. Complete the Post Lab Questions.

Photography Log					
Activity:			Photographer:		
Date:			Location:		
Camera used:				Time start:	Time end:
Photo #	ISO	Aperture	Shutter Speed	Lens	Subject Description

Procedure: Shutter Speed

1. Set digital camera to manual setting; all photographs will be taken in this setting.
2. Set the camera to ISO100 if photographing outdoors; set the camera to ISO400 if photographing indoors.
3. Set the camera's f/stop to its lowest number (f/4, f/5.6, f/8).
4. Set the camera's shutter speed to at least 1/30 or 1/60 to allow hand holding of the camera without camera shake or use of a tripod, and take a photograph of a subject in motion. Record the settings used to capture the image in the provided photography log.
5. Maintain all camera settings except the shutter speed and change it to the camera's highest number (1/500, 1/1000, 1/2000) and take a photograph of the same subject as in step 4. Record the camera settings in the photography log.
6. Compare the two images to visualize the function of shutter speeds.
7. Maintain the camera settings and manipulate only the shutter speed. Photograph the same subject or similar subject using the following range of shutter speeds: 1/4, 1/8, 1/15, 1/30, 1/60, 1/125, 1/500, 1/1000. Record the settings of each photograph. Review your photographs.

Photography Log					
Activity:			Photographer:		
Date:			Location:		
Camera used:				Time start:	Time end:
Photo #	ISO	Aperture	Shutter Speed	Lens	Subject Description

Procedure: Manual Mode

1. Set digital camera to manual setting; all photographs will be taken in this setting.

2. Set the camera to ISO100 if photographing outdoors; set the camera to ISO400 if photographing indoors.

3. Set the camera's shutter speed to at least 1/30 or 1/60.

4. To maximize depth of field, choose one of the following f/stops and set the camera: f/8, f/11, f/16, f/22.

5. Refer to the camera's exposure level scale visible through the viewfinder or on the LCD screen. The camera will indicate a properly metered exposure when the level mark is in the center of the scale.

6. Photograph a subject when a properly exposed image is indicated by the exposure level scale. Record the camera settings in the photography log. Then, manipulate either the shutter speed or f/stop to add one stop of light (level mark on +1) and lose one stop of light (level mark on −1). Record these settings in the photography log.

7. Take photographs of multiple subjects using this method of capturing three photographs of each subject with the level mark at 0, +1, −1. Record all camera settings for each subject in the photography log.

8. Review your photographs to identify deficiencies and take corrective action.

Photography Log					
Activity:			Photographer:		
Date:			Location:		
Camera used:				Time start:	Time end:
Photo #	ISO	Aperture	Shutter Speed	Lens	Subject Description

Post Lab Questions

1. What is the appropriate type of camera to use to document crime scenes?
2. What is depth of field?
3. When shooting an indoor scene, what ISO should be used?
4. What do f/stop numbers refer to?
5. Why is shutter speed important?
6. How can bracketing be useful?
7. Why is oblique lighting useful?

6-2: Capturing Range Photographs

Objectives

- Describe the three basic range photographs.
- Explain the purpose of the crime scene photo log.
- Practice capturing range to include overall, midrange, and closeup photographs.

Materials

- Digital camera
- Writing utensil

Concept Overview

Photography is an essential step in the documentation process. Graphic information is easy to comprehend and shows the real-life context of a crime scene. Photographs and verbal testimony in combination are powerful tools in painting a picture for jurors.

Three basic range photographs are taken to ensure the entire scene is captured. They are overall, midrange, and closeup photographs. Overall photographs depict the general condition and layout of the scene. They should show how the scene is oriented and where major landmarks exist such as street signs and furniture within a room. Midrange photographs are an important key in photographing a scene. Smaller items are often left behind as evidence and are so small they are not visible in overall photographs. Midrange photographs are used to establish the location of the item within the scene by making sure the object is in the frame in conjunction with another scene landmark. This helps to orient it with other items that are present. Closeups of specific items are taken at the closest range possible. Technicians are taught to fill the frame of the camera with the item. The purpose of closeup photographs is to obtain as much detail of the item as possible. These photographs should be taken with and without scale. Scales included in the photos help aid in 1:1 or life-size re-creations of the item. Although photographs are generally taken from the general to the specific, overall closeups, it may be necessary in some cases to alter this protocol. When fragile evidence, such as hairs and fibers, are located at a scene it is important to photograph and collect them as soon as possible. Fragile evidence may be lost or damaged in the course of completing other photographs, which ultimately hurts the investigation.

Photo placards can be used to show the chronological order in which evidentiary items were found and help in evidence identification in overall photographs. The placards may be preprinted, numbers or letters, plastic tents which can be ordered from a number of distributors, or simply folded index cards with numerical or alphabetical notations on them.

Roadmapping is a technique used to photograph bloodstains. It incorporates the three basic photographing techniques (discussed above) in conjunction with a variety of placards and scales in order to accurately reflect the orientation and position of the stains.

The crime scene photo log is an important tool in crime scene photography. The photo log keeps track of each photograph taken and describes what the picture was intended to depict. Photo logs vary in design from simple to very detailed. To be beneficial to the investigation, the log should contain, at the very minimum, the subject matter and exposure number. Additional data such as distance, time, aperture, shutter speed, and any other remarks may also be beneficial to the investigation.

Procedure

1. Set digital camera to Manual setting, if applicable.
2. If applicable,
   - set the camera to ISO 100 if photographing outdoors; set the camera to ISO 400 if photographing indoors.
   - set the camera's shutter speed to at least 1/30 or 1/60 (to prevent camera shake).
   - to maximize depth of field, choose one of the following f/stops and set the camera: f/8, f/11, f/16, f/22.
3. Document the evidentiary items by capturing range photographs to include: overall, midrange, and closeup photographs. Use placards or identifiers and a scale when appropriate.
4. Record all captured images, including the settings used for capture, in the photography log.
5. Complete the Post Lab Questions.

Photography Log					
Activity:			Photographer:		
Date:			Location:		
Camera used.			Time start:		Time end:
Photo #	ISO	Aperture	Shutter Speed	Lens	Subject Description

Post Lab Questions

Picture Number	Strength	Weakness

1. Evaluate twelve of the photographs taken in the exercise above. Describe the strengths and weaknesses of each photograph.
2. Describe the three basic photographs.
3. What is roadmapping?
4. What is the purpose of a photo log?
5. Why might photo placards be especially helpful for jury members?
6. Why is having photographs with and without scale beneficial?

6-3: Documenting a Crime Scene

Objective

- Students will properly document a crime scene utilizing proper photographic methodology.

Materials

- Digital camera
- Writing utensil

Concept Overview

The mock crime scene is the accumulative evaluation of the techniques learned in the previous exercises. It is important to remember the following items when photographing the scene:

- Capture the full range of photographs including overall, midrange, and closeup. Be sure to include scale when necessary.
- Use proper alignment of camera lens with subject. Remember it is important to be perpendicular to the subject.
- Use evidence placards to identify evidence.
- Use proper scale.
- Maximize depth of field.

Procedure

1. If applicable,
   - set digital camera to manual setting.
   - set the camera to ISO100 if photographing outdoors; set the camera to ISO400 if photographing indoors.
   - set the camera's shutter speed to at least 1/30 or 1/60 (to prevent camera shake).
   - to maximize depth of field, choose one of the following f/stops and set the camera: f/8, f/11, f/16, f/22.

2. Document the crime scene using proper photographic methodology to include:
   - capturing range photographs (overall, midrange, closeup)
   - proper alignment of camera lens with subject (perpendicular)
   - proper use of evidence placards or identifiers
   - proper use of scale
   - maximizing depth of field

3. Record all captured images, including the settings used for capture, in the photography log.

4. Complete the Post Lab Questions.

Photography Log

Activity:		Photographer:	
Date:		Location:	

Camera used:	Time start:	Time end:

Photo #	ISO	Aperture	Shutter Speed	Lens	Subject Description

Photography Log

Activity:			Photographer:		
Date:			Location:		

Camera used:				Time start:	Time end:

Photo #	ISO	Aperture	Shutter Speed	Lens	Subject Description

Post Lab Questions

1. What are the four key elements in crime scene documentation?
2. Why is it important to document a crime scene?
3. What is the purpose of bracketing photographs?
4. How can shutter speed affect the resulting photograph?
5. How can one prevent overexposure when using a fill-flash?

Works Cited

Gardner, Ross M. *Practical Crime Scene Processing and Investigations*. Boca Raton, FL: CRC Press, 2005.
Robinson, Edward M. *Crime Scene Photography*. San Diego, CA: Elsevier, 2007.

Crime Scene Sketching and Mapping

Key Terms

Heading
Diagram area
Legend
Title block
Scale of reference
Orientation
Cross-projection sketch
Elevation sketch
Three-dimensional sketch
Rectangular coordinates
Triangulation
Baseline coordinates
Polar coordinates
English measurement system
Metric measurement system

Learning Outcomes

1. Understand the purpose of a crime scene sketch.
2. Identify the five essential elements of a sketch.
3. Review the three views used in crime scene sketching.
4. Identify the four basic methods of mapping a crime scene sketch.

7-1: Measuring with English and Metric Rulers

Objectives

- Explain the difference between the English and metric systems of measurement.
- Practice measuring with English and metric rulers.

Materials

- Writing utensil

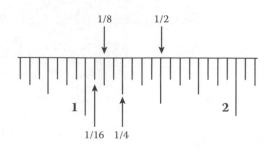

Figure 7.1
One inch ruler broken down in 1/16 increments

Concept Overview

The ability to accurately collect measurements is a crucial skill in crime scene investigation. Collecting incorrect or inaccurate measurements can affect the evidentiary value of scene diagrams and result in erroneous conclusions from shooting incident reconstructions, crime scene reconstructions, and bloodstain pattern analysis. Investigators must be able to use English and metric rulers, each of which is based on very different measurement systems.

The most commonly used measurement system in the United States is the English system, which uses feet and inches for length units. One foot is comprised of twelve inches, and each inch is broken down into fractions. Reading fractions on a ruler can result in erroneous or inaccurate measurements. Figure 7.1 depicts the fractions on a one-inch ruler that is broken down into $\frac{1}{16}$ increments.

The size of the graduations on the ruler vary in size. The largest is in the center or at the halfway point of the one-inch span. This is a $\frac{1}{2}$ inch. The next largest graduation is $\frac{1}{4}$ inch. There are four $\frac{1}{4}$ inch sections per inch since $\frac{1}{4} + \frac{1}{4} + \frac{1}{4} + \frac{1}{4} = 1$ (inch). The next size graduations signify $\frac{1}{8}$ inch. There are eight $\frac{1}{8}$-inch sections per inch since the sum of those sections equals 1 inch. The smallest graduations on the ruler are $\frac{1}{16}$ inch. There are sixteen $\frac{1}{16}$-inch graduations since $\frac{16}{16} = 1$ (inch). Familiarization with fractions is important when reading a ruler because the relationship between the fractions will become clear. For example, examine the equivalent fractions below.

$$\frac{2}{4} = \frac{1}{2}$$
$$\frac{2}{8} = \frac{1}{4}$$
$$\frac{4}{8} = \frac{1}{2}$$
$$\frac{6}{8} = \frac{3}{4}$$
$$\frac{2}{16} = \frac{1}{8}$$
$$\frac{4}{16} = \frac{1}{4}$$
$$\frac{6}{16} = \frac{3}{8}$$
$$\frac{8}{16} = \frac{1}{2}$$
$$\frac{10}{16} = \frac{5}{8}$$
$$\frac{12}{16} = \frac{3}{4}$$
$$\frac{14}{16} = \frac{7}{8}$$

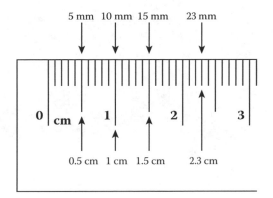

Figure 7.2
Metric ruler in centimeters

The fraction on the left was simplified by dividing the numerator (top number) and denominator (bottom number) by the highest number that can divide evenly into both numbers. If a person lacks experience in reading rulers, it is best to count each graduation or mark on the ruler to derive the measurement; then, if necessary, simplify the resulting fraction. Soon, experience will lead to quicker, accurate measurement determinations.

The metric system, in comparison with the English system, is much simpler. Fractions are not used. Rather, in this system, there is multiplication or division by ten to move between units of length. Metric units of length are the meter, centimeter, and millimeter. On a ruler, the units are typically centimeters and millimeters. One centimeter is comprised of ten millimeters (Figure 7.2).

Thus, 4 centimeters (cm) is the equivalent of 40 millimeters (mm). Sixty millimeters is equal to 6 cm, while 6 mm is equal to 0.6 cm. Because movement between the unit lengths is a function of base ten and results by moving the decimal point, this is considered a decimal system. For any given number, the decimal point is moved to the right for larger units of length and moved to the left for smaller units of length.

It is important to be familiar with this measurement system because some types of evidence are, as a rule, measured in metric. Examples of such evidence are bloodstains and bullet strikes, which are measured in millimeters.

Procedure

1. Use the rulers provided in this manual to measure the practice figures with the English and metric systems of measurement.
2. Record your measurements in the *Data Worksheet*.
3. The instructor will confirm your measurements.
4. Complete the Post Lab Questions.

Practice Figures

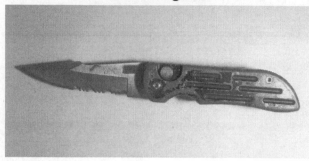

Figure 7.3
Knife
_____ cm
_____ mm
_____ inches

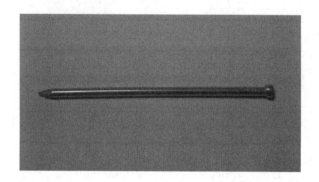

Figure 7.4
Nail
_____ cm
_____ mm
_____ inches

Figure 7.5
Fired cartridge case
_____ cm
_____ mm
_____ inches

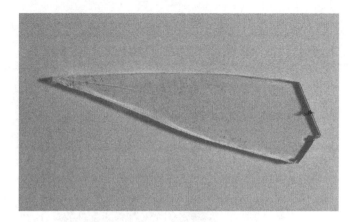

Figure 7.6
Broken piece of glass
_____ cm
_____ mm
_____ inches

Figure 7.7
Bullet
_____ cm
_____ mm
_____ inches

Figure 7.8
Shoe print

_____ cm
_____ mm
_____ inches

Data Worksheet

Object	English measurement (inches)	Metric measurement (cm and mm)
Knife		
Nail		
Fired cartridge case		
Broken piece of glass		
Bullet		
Shoe print		

Post Lab Questions

1. What is the base unit of the metric unit?
2. How many centimeters are in 125 ¾ inches?
3. Convert each of the measurements:

4 inches	centimeters
35 inches	millimeters
78 ½ inches	centimeters
520 centimeters	millimeters
400 millimeters	inches

4. Find the lowest common denominator.

16/48	
3/9	
48/120	
14/16	
20/32	

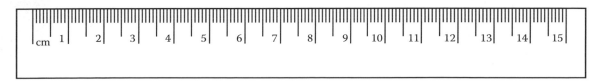

Figure 7.9
English ruler

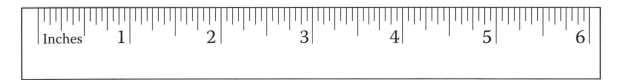

Figure 7.10
Metric ruler

7-2: Creating an Outdoor Sketch

Objective

- Students will use the appropriate mapping method to create a sketch of an outdoor area.

Materials

- Writing utensil

Concept Overview

Crime scene sketching and mapping, together, create a picture of the crime scene. A sketch is the actual drawing itself, while crime scene mapping is the technique chosen to measure and document the elements within the scene. All sketches should contain five essential elements:

- Heading: Information that indicates the purpose of the sketch.
- Diagram area: The drawing itself.
- Legend: Indicates what various labels (usually numbers or letters) represent.
- Title block: Area that provides important information relevant to the location of the scene and its creator.
- Scale and direction notation: Scale notes the scale of reference that was used in the sketch. If no scale was used, it should note that the sketch is "not drawn to scale." Direction notation suggests the compass direction.

A rough sketch begins the process. Rough sketches contain *all* the measurements within the scene. It is usually done on standard white paper or graph paper and drawn in pencil. A title block, legend, and scale and direction should be noted on the rough sketch as well. Final sketches occur in a variety of formats. Hand-drawn sketches are completed in pen on white paper or graph paper, while computer-generated final sketches may appear in a range of formats.

Variations on the view or perspective of the sketch can provide the creator with the option to use the one that is most beneficial for viewing the scene. Three common perspective variations are cross-projection or exploded, elevation, and three-dimensional sketches. The standard cross-projection sketch provides a bird's eye view of the crime scene. The exploded cross-projection sketch provides a bird's eye view of the scene, while at the same time laying down the walls. This would allow any evidentiary items, such as bullet strikes or blood evidence, located on the walls or other vertical surfaces to be oriented and to indicate their interrelationship with other items at the scene in a plain and understandable way. The elevation sketch is a drawing depicting a side view of some portion of the scene, typically an interior wall or similar vertical structure. The three-dimensional sketch offers the ability to present the crime scene in a realistic perspective or as the human eye sees it. These sketches are generally produced using software and they allow the jury to get a real feel for the scene.

Mapping the scene is the act of taking measurements of all items within the scene and documenting them. This is also known as plotting or fixing evidence. There are four basic techniques for mapping a scene:

1. Rectangular coordinates: This method is best suited for crime scenes with clear and specific boundaries such as walls. It is a good method for interior crime scenes and can be a fast and effective manner of measuring. The rectangular coordinates mapping technique only requires two measurements from any item within the scene. The procedure for plotting evidence with rectangular coordinates is as follows.

    a. Choose two fixed reference points (typically walls). All measurements will be taken from these points. These measurements may be thought of as *x* and *y* coordinates.

    b. Each item of evidence is plotted separately. Choose a location on the fixed point (wall) that is near the evidentiary item. Keep the end of the tape (metal hook) in contact with the fixed point (wall) while the tape is pulled out until reaching the item. Ensure the tape measure is perpendicular or 90 degrees from the fixed point to the item. Record the measurement.

    c. From the second fixed point (wall), repeat this procedure. (Through this mapping method, two perpendicular lines are created and used to plot items.)

    d. Whether or not to include these measurements on a finished sketch depends on the complexity of the scene and the number of items or objects mapped.

2. Triangulation: This method is very effective in "fixing" items in the crime scene. The number of measurements taken is determined by whether the item being measured is regular (definite/defined sides or edges) or irregular (amorphous). Items that are regular will not change shape with movement and require a minimum of four measurements. Examples of regularly shaped items are furniture in a room and a gun. Irregularly shaped items have an asymmetric shape with no definable shape and would change shape with movement. Irregularly shaped items require two measurements from two fixed objects in the room to the center mass of the object being measured. An example is an article of clothing. Triangulation is a useful tool when the sketch creator wants to fix items within the crime scene. However, the method can be very time consuming and typically requires more than one person to obtain the measurements. The procedure for plotting evidence with rectangular coordinates is as follows:

    a. Locate two fixed (permanent) objects (door frames, room corners).

    b. Keep the end of the tape (metal hook) in contact with the fixed point while the tape is pulled out until reaching the item to be plotted. For regular objects, the measurement will be taken at a corner or edge. For irregular objects, the measurement will be taken at center mass. Record the measurement.

    c. From the second fixed or permanent point, repeat this procedure.

    d. Record the distance between the two fixed points. (This is the base of the triangle. With all measurements recorded, a triangle has been created.)

    e. A separate triangle is formed for each item or object mapped.

    f. Whether or not to include these measurements on a finished sketch depends on the complexity of the scene and the number of items or objects mapped.

3. Baseline coordinates: This method is best utilized for outdoor scenes without evident landmarks. Typically, a general search of an area has been conducted and items of possible evidentiary value have been located. Such discovery assists in productive, efficient placement of the baseline. First, a datum point is established and the baseline is extended in one cardinal direction (north, south, east, or west). A soft (vinyl) measuring tape is the best tool to use as the baseline. The procedure for plotting evidence with baseline coordinates is as follows:

    a. Each item of evidence is plotted separately. When an item is located *along* the baseline, a measurement along the soft tape is recorded. (This can be considered the *x* coordinate.)

    b. A second measuring device is used to determine the object's distance *from* the baseline (soft tape). (This can be considered the *y* coordinate.)

    c. The object's direction from the baseline should also be recorded. (For example, if the baseline is oriented in a west to east direction, the plotted item will either be north or south of the baseline.)

    d. Repeat this procedure for each item or object mapped.

4. Polar coordinates: This method is used in mapping exterior scenes where evidence is scattered over a large, relatively open area. It is not effective in heavily wooded areas or where large obstacles may block the line of sight. Polar coordinates are based on surveying techniques and are generally conducted by personnel who are trained in the technique.

    Sketching is a critical form of documentation. Sketches supplement photographs and notes taken at the crime scene. Together, they provide a comprehensive view of the scene for a jury and allow the jury to view the interrelationship of evidence and items located within the crime scene.

Procedure

1. Create a rough sketch of an outdoor area using a projection view. Use the blank *Sketch Canvas* provided. The mapping method will be *baseline coordinates*. Use the *Mapping Measurement Record* to assist you with measurement data collection. For the purpose of *baseline coordinate* sketches, the *x* measurement should notate the measurement located along the baseline of the measuring tape. The *y* measurement should notate the distance the object is from the baseline.

2. Submit your rough sketch to the instructor for evaluation.

3. After the rough sketch is approved, create a finished sketch, on the *Sketch Canvas* (graph paper) provided, for submission that includes the necessary elements:

   Heading
   Diagram area
   Legend
   Title block
   Scale of reference
   Direction orientation

4. Submit your finished sketch to the instructor for evaluation.

5. Complete the Post Lab Questions.

Sketch Canvas

Mapping Measurement Record: Baseline Coordinates

Sketch artist: Date:

Location:

Placard #	Object	Compass direction from baseline	X measurement	Y measurement

Sketch Canvas

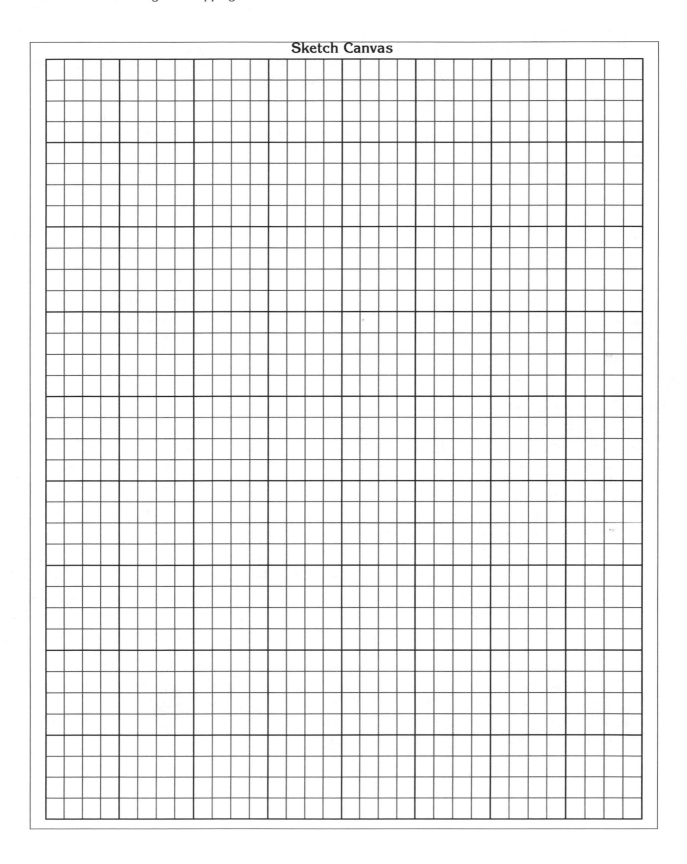

Post Lab Questions

1. Was the baseline method of mapping easy to use? Why or why not?
2. What are the five key elements of a crime scene sketch? Name and describe each.
3. How might a sketch be beneficial in courtroom testimony?
4. When would an elevation sketch be used? Give an example.
5. Define a cross-projection sketch.

7-3: Creating an Sketch

Objective

- Students will use the appropriate mapping method to create a sketch of an area.

Materials

- Writing utensil

Concept Overview

Crime scene sketching and mapping, together, create a picture of the crime scene. A sketch is the actual drawing itself while crime scene mapping is the technique chosen to measure and document the elements within the scene. All sketches should contain five essential elements:

- Heading: Information that indicates the purpose of the sketch.
- Diagram area: The drawing itself.
- Legend: Indicates what various labels are representing.
- Title block: Area that provides important information relevant to the location of the scene and its creator.
- Scale and direction notation: Scale notes the scale of reference that was used in the sketch. If no scale was used, it should note that the sketch is "not drawn to scale." Direction notation suggests the compass direction.

A rough sketch begins the process. Rough sketches contain *all* the measurements within the scene. It is usually done on standard white paper and written in pencil. A title block, legend, and scale and direction should be noted on the rough sketch as well. Final sketches occur in a variety of formats. Hand-drawn sketches are completed in pen and on graph paper, while computer-generated final sketches may appear in a range of formats.

Variations on the view of the sketch can provide the creator with the option to complete the view that will be most beneficial to the case. Three common variations are cross-projection or exploded cross-projection, elevation, and three-dimensional. The standard cross-projection sketch provides a bird's eye view of the crime scene. The exploded cross-projection sketch provides a bird's eye view of the scene, while at the same time laying down the walls. This would allow any evidentiary items located on the walls or other vertical surfaces to be oriented and their interrelationship with other items at the scene exposed. The elevation sketch is a drawing depicting a side view of some portion of the scene, typically an interior wall or similar vertical structure. The three-dimensional sketch offers the ability to present the crime scene in a realistic prospective. These sketches are generally produced using software to allow the jury to get a real feel for the scene.

Mapping the scene is the act of taking measurements of all items within the scene and documenting them. There are four basic techniques for mapping a scene:

1. Rectangular coordinates: This method is best suited for crime scenes with clear and specific boundaries such as walls. It is a good fit for interior crime scenes and can be a fast and effective form of measuring. The rectangular coordinates mapping technique only requires two measurements from any item within the scene. Although the measurements document the location of the item, the item could still be rotated 360 degrees, therefore it is not fixed within the scene.

2. Triangulation: This method is very effective in "fixing" items in the crime scene. Measurements are taken based on whether the item being measured is regular or irregular. Items that are regular will not change shape with movement and require a minimum of four measurements. Examples of regularly shaped items are furniture in a room and a gun. Irregularly shaped items have an asymmetric shape with no definable shape and would change shape with movement. Irregularly shaped items require two measurements from two fixed objects to the center mass of the object being measured. Triangulation is a useful tool when the sketch creator wants to fix items within the crime scene. However, the method can be very time consuming.

3. Baseline coordinates: This method is best utilized for outdoor scenes without evident landmarks, although it can also be used indoors. In an exterior scene, a datum point is established and the baseline is extended in one cardinal direct (north, south, east, or west). The best method for creating a baseline is to use an actual measuring tape. If this is not available, a long piece of string or line with reference points is suitable.

4. Polar coordinates: This method is used in mapping exterior scenes where evidence is scattered over a large, relatively open area. It is not effective in heavily wooded areas or where large obstacles may block the line of sight. Polar coordinates are based on surveying techniques and are generally conducted by personnel who are trained in the technique.

Overall, sketching is an important form of documentation. It is created to supplement photographs and notes taken at the crime scene. It gives the jury the opportunity to view the interrelationship of other evidence and items located within the crime scene.

Procedure

1. Create a rough sketch of an indoor area using either a projection or cross-projection view. Use the blank *Sketch Canvas* provided. The mapping method will either be assigned by the instructor or you will choose to use either *rectangular coordinates or triangulation*. Use the *Mapping Measurement Record* to assist you with measurement data collection.
2. Submit your rough sketch to the instructor for evaluation.
3. After the rough sketch is approved, create a finished sketch, on the *Sketch Canvas* (graph paper) provided, for submission that includes the necessary elements:

   Heading
   Diagram area
   Legend
   Title block
   Scale of reference
   Direction orientation

4. Submit your finished sketch to the instructor for evaluation.
5. Complete the Post Lab Questions.

Sketch Canvas

Mapping Measurement Record: Rectangular Coordinates			
Sketch artist:		Date:	
Location:			
Placard #	Object	X measurement	Y measurement

Mapping Measurement Record: Triangulation						
Sketch artist:				Date:		
Location:						
Placard #	R or IR	Object	RP-1	RP-2	RP-3	RP-4

Sketch Canvas

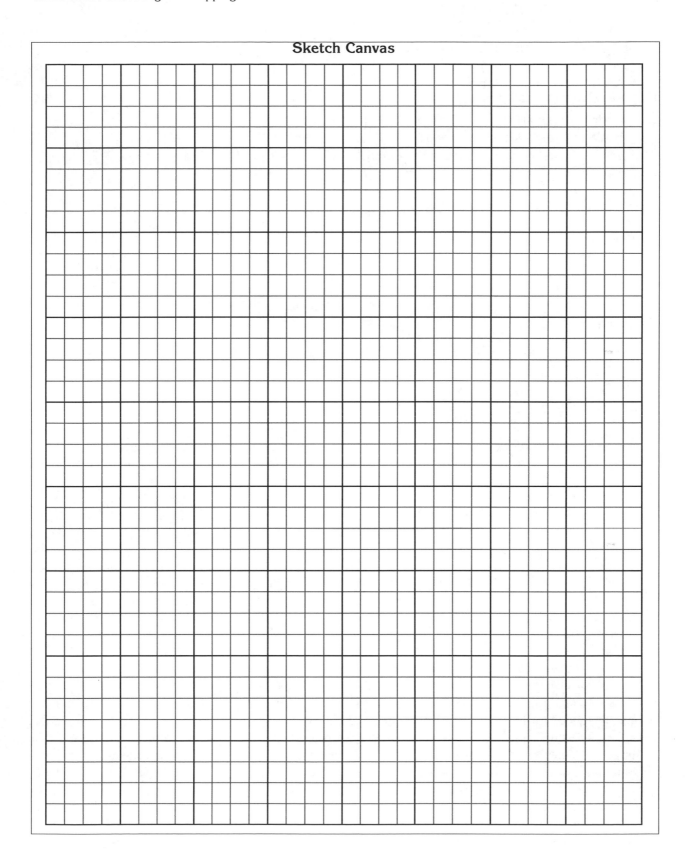

Post Lab Questions

1. After using both rectangular coordinates and triangulation, which measuring method was easier to use? Explain.
2. Why is triangulation considered a more accurate form of measuring?
3. In what type of scene are baseline coordinate measurements best implemented?
4. Why is accuracy in sketching important?
5. What are some challenges to completing a crime scene sketch outdoors?

7-4: Sketching a Crime Scene

Objective

- Students will use the appropriate mapping method to sketch a crime scene.

Materials

- Writing utensil

Concept Overview

Crime scene sketching and mapping, together, create a picture of the crime scene. A sketch is the actual drawing itself, while crime scene mapping is the technique chosen to measure and document the elements within the scene. All sketches should contain five essential elements:

- Heading: Information that indicates the purpose of the sketch.
- Diagram area: The drawing itself.
- Legend: Indicates what various labels are representing.
- Title block: Area that provides important information relevant to the location of the scene and its creator.
- Scale and direction notation: Scale notes the scale of reference that was used in the sketch. If no scale was used, it should note that the sketch is "not drawn to scale." Direction notation suggests the compass direction.

A rough sketch begins the process. Rough sketches contain *all* the measurements within the scene. It is usually done on standard white paper and written in pencil. A title block, legend, and scale and direction should be noted on the rough sketch as well. Final sketches occur in a variety of formats. Hand-drawn sketches are completed in pen and on graph paper, while computer-generated final sketches may appear in a range of formats.

Variations on the view of the sketch can provide the creator with the option to complete the view that is most beneficial to the case. Three common variations are cross-projection or exploded cross-projection, elevation, and three-dimensional. The standard cross-projection sketch provides a bird's eye view of the crime scene. The exploded cross-projection sketch provides a bird's eye view of the scene, while at the same time laying down the walls. This would allow any evidentiary items located on the walls or other vertical surfaces to be oriented and their interrelationship with other items at the scene exposed. The elevation sketch is a drawing depicting a side view of some portion of the scene, typically an interior wall or similar vertical structure. The three-dimensional sketch offers the ability to present the crime scene in a realistic prospective. These sketches are generally produced using software, which allows the jury to get a real feel for the scene.

Mapping the scene is the act of taking measurements of all items within the scene and documenting them. There are four basic techniques for mapping a scene:

1. Rectangular coordinates: This method is best suited for crime scenes with clear and specific boundaries such as walls. It is a good fit for interior crime scenes and can be a fast and effective form of measuring. The rectangular coordinates mapping technique only requires two measurements from any item within the scene. Although the measurements document the location of the item, the item could still be rotated 360 degrees, therefore it is not fixed within the scene.

2. Triangulation: This method is very effective in "fixing" items in the crime scene. Measurements are taken based on whether the item being measured is regular or irregular. Items that are regular will not change shape with movement and require a minimum of four measurements. Examples of regularly shaped items are furniture in a room and a gun. Irregularly shaped items have an asymmetric shape with no definable shape and would change shape with movement. Irregularly shaped items require two measurements from two fixed objects in the room to the center mass of the object being measured. Triangulation is a useful tool when the sketch creator wants to fix items within the crime scene. However, the method can be very time consuming.

3. Baseline coordinates: This method is best utilized for outdoor scenes without evident landmarks, although it can also be used indoors. In an exterior scene, a datum point is established and the baseline is extended in one cardinal direct (north, south, east, or west). The best method for creating a baseline is to use an actual measuring tape. If this is not available, a long piece of string or line with reference points is suitable.

4. Polar coordinates: This method is used in mapping exterior scenes where evidence is scattered over a large, relatively open area. It is not effective in heavily wooded areas or where large obstacles may block the line of sight. Polar coordinates are based on surveying techniques and are generally conducted by personnel who are trained in the technique.

Overall, sketching is an important form of documentation. It is created to supplement photographs and notes taken at the crime scene. It gives the jury the opportunity to view the interrelationship of other evidence and items located within the crime scene.

Procedure

1. Create a rough sketch of the scene presented by the instructor. The view of the scene should be through a projection sketch or cross-projection sketch. Use the blank *Sketch Canvas* provided. The mapping method utilized will be indicated by the instructor, or you will choose the appropriate method based on the scene location: *rectangular coordinates or triangulation (indoors) or baseline coordinates (outdoors)*. Use the *Mapping Measurement Record* to assist you with measurement data collection.
2. Submit your rough sketch to the instructor for evaluation.
3. After the rough sketch is approved, create a finished sketch, on the *Sketch Canvas* (graph paper) provided, for submission that includes the necessary elements:

   Heading
   Diagram area
   Legend
   Title block
   Scale of reference
   Direction orientation

4. Submit your finished sketch to the instructor for evaluation.
5. Complete the Post Lab Questions.

Sketch Canvas

Mapping Measurement Record: Rectangular Coordinates			
Sketch artist:		Date:	
Location:			
Placard #	Object	X measurement	Y measurement

Mapping Measurement Record: Triangulation						
Sketch artist:			Date:			
Location:						
Placard #	R or IR	Object	RP-1	RP-2	RP-3	RP-4

Mapping Measurement Record: Baseline Coordinates				
Sketch artist:			Date:	
Location:				
Placard #	Object	Compass direction from baseline	X measurement	Y measurement

Sketch Canvas

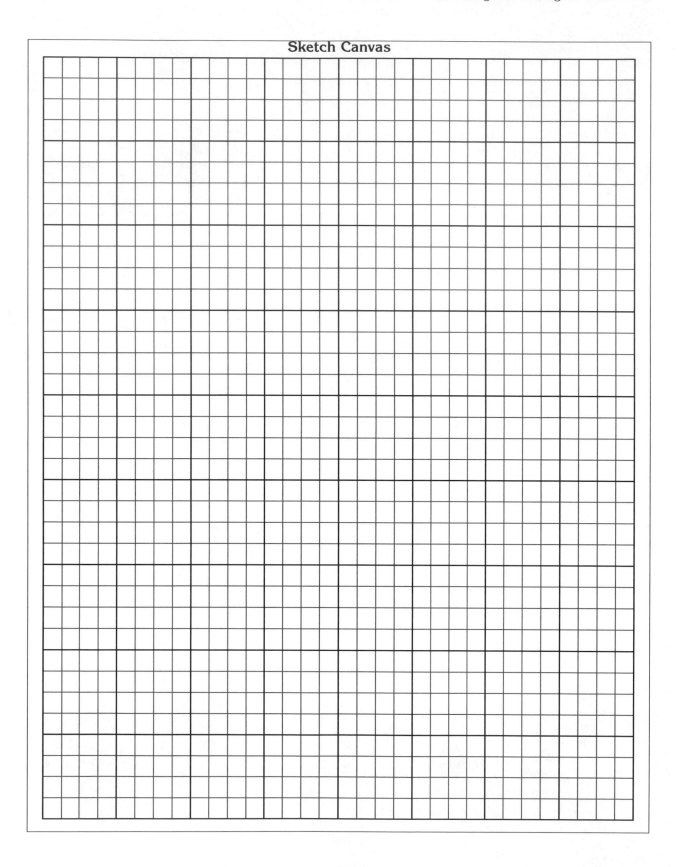

Post Lab Questions

1. Were you systematic and methodical in sketching the scene provided?
2. How might multiple people assisting in the sketching of the scene be beneficial? How might it be problematic?
3. How is the rough sketch different from the finished sketch?
4. Could a baseline sketch be used at an indoor crime scene? Why or why not?
5. What was the easiest form of measurement, inches, centimeters, or millimeters? Explain.

Works Cited

Gardner, Ross M. *Practical Crime Scene Processing and Investigation.* Boca Raton, FL: CRC Press, 2005.

8

Narrative Descriptions
Crime Scene Notes and Reports

Key Terms

Introduction
Characteristics of the scene
Conditions of the scene
Environmental conditions
Entry and exit points
Scene documentation

Learning Outcomes

1. Identify three characteristics shared by crime scene notes and a crime scene report.

2. Explain how crime scene notes support the long-term investigation.

3. Determine three items a crime scene report should *not* contain.

4. Explain the necessity of creating a methodical and ordered crime scene report.

8-1: Creating a Field Note Document Template

Objective

- Students are to create a field note document template to serve as the framework for crime scene report narratives.

Materials

- Writing utensil

Concept Overview

Crime scene notes and reports are the narrative form of documentation pertinent to all cases. The mission of the crime scene technician is to create notes and a report that are detailed, accurate, and understandable. Crime scene notes are the cornerstone of all investigations. They should reflect an accurate description of all observations and actions taken at the scene. Ultimately, this accumulation of relevant facts, observations, and actions should be organized and placed in a final report. The crime scene report should *not* contain a cursory discussion of only the focal points found within the crime scene. Rather, the scene and its evidence should be described in adequate detail to relay the important characteristics of the scene and the interrelationships of the evidence within the scene. A crime scene report should also not be a narrative stating why the suspect is guilty. Crime scene reports should stay focused on the scene investigation, the evidence of the scene, and the provable facts. Crime scene reports should not solely contain descriptions of evidence limited to those that support a hypothesis. Instead, reports should contain unbiased information concerning all physical evidence of the scene and evidence related to the investigation, regardless of whether that evidence is in support or direct opposition of investigative theories.

A crime scene report should be organized; this can be difficult when faced with a complex crime scene. The following format is suggested for addressing all necessary information. The format may be altered based on the complexity of the scene.

- Introduction
  - Who worked the scene, location, date, time, reason for the examination.
- Characteristics of the scene
  - General description of the area and associated features such as doors, windows, geographic features (exterior scenes). These are static and stable items that will not change.
- Conditions of the scene
  - Specific conditions that pertain to the investigation such as cleanliness, level of disarray, and descriptions of evidentiary items.
- Environmental conditions
  - Weather or scene conditions noted at the time of the investigation.
- Factors relevant to entry and exit
  - Addresses both known and possible avenues of entering and departing the scene.
- Scene documentation
  - Describes the basic efforts taken to photograph and sketch the scene. This may include equipment used and how the documentation was created.
- Collection of physical evidence
  - A description of all physical evidence located in the scene. If an evidence log has been created, a cross reference may be used.
- Search for latent prints
  - Describes the areas that were processed for latent prints and both their positive and negative results.
- Additional examinations
- This area is dependent on the type of crime scene that is present. Examinations may include but are not limited to fire patterns at an arson scene or bloodstain patterns at a violent crime scene.

Procedure

1. Examine the subjects/categories in the *Data Worksheet.*

2. In the *Field Note Document Template Outline*, place the subjects and categories in the appropriate sections:
   - Introduction
   - Characteristics of the scene
   - Conditions of the scene
   - Environmental conditions
   - Factors pertinent to entry and exit
   - Scene documentation
   - Collection of physical evidence
   - Search for latent prints
   - Additional examinations

3. Maintaining the order of the nine section format, create a field note template.

4. Complete the Post Lab Questions.

Data Worksheet

Field Note Subjects/Categories	
Time en route	Doors/windows secured
Designated diagram area for sketching decedent	Marbling
Type of camera used to capture photographs	Indoor vs. outdoor scene
Bloodstain pattern analysis	Outdoor temperature
Success in fingerprint development and location of development	Seized vehicles
Collected clothing	Interior scene lighting
Offense/investigation type	Jewelry
Footwear/tire tracks	Location
Ambient temperature of interior scene	Trajectory analysis
Collected gunshot residue (GSR) kit	Petechial hemorrhaging
Creation and inclusion of photography log	Notified by
Available light: dawn, dusk, daylight, night	Thermostat setting
Decomposition	Collected DNA samples
Videotaping (type of camera used)	Investigator
Construction of indoor scene: brick, wood, metal, other	Development methods used
Weather: foggy, clear, cloudy, rainy, sunny	Rigor mortis
Collected blood evidence samples	Creation of rough sketches
Physical description of decedent	Time notified
Use of specialty equipment, i.e., alternate light source	Clothing
Descriptors of outdoor scene: wooded, partially wooded, open field	Position of decedent
Presence/absence of forced entry	Lividity
Collected fingernail scrapings/cuttings	Date
Presence of pry marks/tool marks	Exterior lighting and type
Compass direction indoor scene facing	Wounds
No success in fingerprint development	Time arrived
Type of structure: home, mobile home, business	Scars
Use of special photography techniques	Time arrived
Collected combed/pulled head hair	Insect/animal activity
Side of roadway indoor scene located	Blanching
Documentation of developed fingerprints/palm prints	Tattoos
Collected firearms/firearm evidence	Skin slippage
Chemical enhancement methods employed	
Exterior color of indoor scene: primary and trim	
Areas examined for fingerprints/palm prints	
Distance from roadway of indoor scene	
No success in fingerprint development	
Exterior descriptors of indoor scene location	

Field Note Document Template Outline

Section 1: Introduction

Section 2: Characteristics of the Scene

Section 3: Conditions of the Scene

Section 4: Environmental Conditions

Section 5: Factors Pertinent to Entry and Exit

Section 6: Scene Documentation

Section 7: Collection of Physical Evidence

Section 8: Search for Latent Prints

Section 9: Additional Examinations

Post Lab **Questions**

1. What should a crime scene report *not* contain?
2. How might the template created help when taking notes at a crime scene?
3. Describe the difference between the characteristics and conditions of the scene.
4. Why is an Introduction important to begin a report?
5. What three characteristics should a good narrative display?

Works Cited

Gardner, Ross M. *Practical Crime Scene Processing and Investigation.* Boca Raton, FL: CRC Press, 2005.

Chapter 9

Basic Skills for Scene Processing

Key Terms

Latent
Substrate
Patent
Plastic
Porous
Nonporous
Cyanoacrylate ester
Fuming tank
Impression
Alternate light source
Electromagnetic spectrum
Nanometer
Reflection
Absorption
Transmission
Conversion
Luminescence
Fluorescence
Phosphorescence
Barrier glasses/shields
Diopters

Learning Outcomes

1. Identify the four basic surface characteristics that help define the method used to fingerprint process those surface types.
2. Execute techniques involving powder/brush processing, cyanoacrylate ester fuming, and chemical processing for print development.
3. Identify the primary techniques of recovering fingerprint impression evidence.

9-1: Cyanoacrylate Ester Fuming and Fingerprint Powder Exercise

Objectives

- Develop good techniques for processing and lifting latent prints using cyanoacrylate ester fuming and black powder techniques.
- Understand the principles regarding cyanoacrylate ester fuming.
- Practice both black powder processing and superglue fuming with subsequent black powder processing techniques, using various brush/powder combinations on the objects and surfaces provided.

Materials

- Writing utensil

Concept Overview

There are three types of fingerprint impressions: latent, patent, and plastic. The term *latent* means hidden or invisible. This type of print requires assistance, such as powder or chemical application, for visualization. Fingerprint and friction ridge skin impressions are developable because contact between friction skin surfaces and a substrate can result in residue deposits. The components of the deposits from friction ridge skin are water (98 percent) and nonorganic compounds, salt, amino acids, and oil (2 percent combined). The nonorganic components of the residue are the targets of the development reagents employed. All developed prints should be photographed, when possible, prior to any attempts of lifting as the lifting process may result in a partial lift or destruction of the print without any success in lifting. The preservation of prints developed through chemical means is photography; these prints cannot be lifted with tape.

There are occasions when the residue deposit is very heavy. The use of reflective lighting can allow for discovery of areas contacted on a substrate (an object on which a print is deposited). If such areas are discovered, the processor can determine an area to begin the development process. Reflective lighting is a powerful yet simple tool that can be used on objects that have a reflective quality. The light source of a room, such as an overhead light fixture, is used for this technique. Although any type of light will suffice, fluorescent lighting is best. The substrate is held, with gloved hands, by its corners and edges and moved in a variety of directions to allow the overhead light to fall on it. The falling light will reflect on the object's surface and may reveal latent impressions.

Patent prints are those that are visible to the unaided eye. This visibility is due to a contaminant on the friction ridge skin such as grease, paint, or blood. Although patent prints are visible without processing, enhancement chemicals may be applied for additional development or better visualization. Enhancement chemicals applied to bloody prints react to the heme or protein of the blood. Preservation of these prints is documented through photography; they cannot be lifted with tape.

Plastic prints are visible impressions in pliable or malleable substrates such as soap or wax. Preservation of these prints is through photography; they cannot be lifted with tape.

Fingerprints can be found on a variety of medium that are divided into six categories:

- Porous: Paper products such as cardboard and untreated wood.
- Nonporous smooth: Finished or painted surfaces such as glass and the majority of plastics
- Nonporous rough: Textured surfaces such as vinyl or leather
- Adhesive: Items which contain a matte and/or "sticky" side
- Special conditions/surfaces: Processing bloody prints or human skin

Each surface has a unique set of challenges. It is important to practice different techniques on various types of surfaces to be prepared for any type of crime scene processing.

Black powder processing is the most common type of fingerprint processing. This straight-forward technique uses a brush and black powder to help visualize and obtain latent prints for analysis. However, developing a viable fingerprint is more difficult than one would think. Several problems can arise when processing for latent prints, such as overpowdering of the latent print or using too much pressure when dusting for a latent print. Latent prints are delicate and can be easily damaged. It is very important to practice dusting for prints prior to working a crime scene. The application method for black powder is as follows:

1. Ensure the fingerprint brush is clean and free of debris via visual examination.
2. Separate the brush bristles by spinning the brush.
3. Pour a small amount of powder onto a clean piece of paper.
4. Lightly tap the brush bristles into the powder.
5. Remove excess powder from the bristles by shaking the brush.
6. Apply powder to the item by twirling the brush in a circular motion (Figure 9.1).
7. When ridge detail appears, apply powder by moving the brush in the direction of the print's visible ridge flow (Figure 9.2).
8. Continue to develop the print until maximum contrast is reached (Figure 9.3). Surpassing maximum contrast will result in visible degradation of the print.

Magnetic brush and powder is a fairly new alternative to standard brush and powder techniques. The magnetic brush is composed of a magnetic rod that is covered by a sheath. The black powder is composed of the same elements with the addition of metallic shavings. This technique is just as effective as the standard brush and powder but eliminates some of the mess. The magnetic powder is applied to the end of the brush, creating a bulb of powder. The powder is then lightly applied across the print and the remaining powder

Figure 9.1
Powder application—brush in circular motion

Figure 9.2
Brush motion follows ridge flow of developing print

Figure 9.3
Developed print at maximum contrast

deposited back into the container. This helps to limit excessive powdering and reuse unused powder. The application method for magnetic powder is as follows:

1. Place the tip of the magnetic wand into the magnetic powder.
2. The magnetic powder will adhere to the magnet within the sheath of the wand to create the "brush."
3. Apply the powder to the item by moving the brush in a circular motion. (Only the powder should contact the item, not the bulb of the sheath. Contacting the wand to the item will destroy the print.)
4. When ridge detail appears, apply powder by moving the brush in the direction of the print's visible ridge flow.
5. Continue to develop the print until maximum contrast is reached. Surpassing maximum contrast will result in visible degradation of the print.

Camel hair brushes and marabou feather brushes may also be used. Camel hair provides a much stiffer brush and is generally used for cleaning off excess powder that has been applied to the print. Caution must be used when utilizing this brush. The stiff bristles, if used incorrectly, may damage or destroy delicate prints. Marabou feather brushes are a much lighter form and should be used on delicate prints when fiberglass or camel hair is too abrasive. An example of when a feather brush should be used would be to remove soot off a medium containing an etched print covered in soot from a fire. Using any type of fingerprint brush is a skill that must be practiced. Employing one of the brushes discussed without proper training and practice could be detrimental to a case.

Cyanoacrylate ester fuming (CA fuming), also known as *superglue fuming*, is a technique commonly used to stabilize or harden the print in order for more rigorous processes to be conducted. CA fuming is conducted using an enclosed area such as a fish tank or cardboard box, a heating medium such as a hot plate, a small container of warm water to produce the humidity needed in the reaction, and a small bottle of liquid superglue. Once the item has been placed in the enclosed area, superglue is placed on the heating element and a chemical reaction takes place. This reaction causes the polymerization of the fingerprint, which allows it to become hardened and stable for further processing. Do not overfume items, as overfuming will prevent powder from adhering to the prints. Overpowdered prints will be white in color and appear heavily coated. Caution should be used to avoid inhaling CA fumes. Before removing items from the tank, vent it by slightly canting the tank lid to allow fumes to escape. After removing objects from the tank's interior, turn the heating element off. To preserve prints developed with powders, lifting tape and lifting cards are used. There are various sizes of tape, ranging from 1-inch to 4-inch rolls. Each tape width brings its own difficulties. It is important to practice with various sizes and be comfortable with each. Processors should never use tape with which they are unfamiliar or have never used at a crime scene. Lifting prints is an art and is a skill that must be honed. The method for lifting prints is as follows:

1. If the top layer of tape is dirty or smudged with powder, remove it in order to lift with clean tape.
2. Create a "handle" at the end of the tape by folding a half-inch piece of the tape on itself. Students can avoid depositing their fingerprints on the adhesive side of the tape by only touching the handle and tape roll.
3. Anchor the tape (handle side) to the surface of the item 1 inch beyond the developed print.
4. Hold the tape roll up at a slight angle and apply the lifting tape over the print by using the index finger. Smooth the tape down onto the item's surface by moving your index finger through the print toward the tape roll.
5. Eliminate air bubbles by rubbing over them with items such as an index card or eraser.
6. Use the tape roll to begin lifting the tape from the surface until reaching the handle and lifting the tape completely from the item's surface.
7. Using a card large enough to hold the developed print, anchor the handle side of the lifting tape onto the lift card. Smooth the tape down onto the card by using the index finger to move across the tape and toward the tape roll.
8. After applying the tape to the lift card, create another handle. With the handle pressed firmly against the tape roll, tear the tape. This allows the handle to stay attached to the roll and ready for immediate use.

After the lifting tape has been placed on the lift card, information must be written on the back side of the card for documentation. This information includes:

- Name of processor
- Date/time
- Location from which the print was collected (object/substrate)
- Offense, case number, or title information provided by instructor

A diagram must also be created on the back of the card. The diagram depicts the object that was processed, and an X is placed on the diagram to illustrate the location on the object from which the print was collected. On the front of the card (print side), an arrow is drawn to indicate the orientation of the print (Figure 9.4).

Challenges involving large prints such as full palm prints or footprints are regularly encountered. When lifting large impressions such as these, strips of tape are used until the entire area is covered. The key to using multiple strips is overlapping them by at least a quarter inch. After covering the entire impression area, lift all tape strips simultaneously and apply to an appropriately sized backing card or a piece of paper or card stock.

Black powder, magnetic powder processing, and CA fuming are the cornerstones of crime scene processing. It is important to use this exercise to help you develop good processing skills.

Front of Lift Card

Back of Lift Card

Figure 9.4
Front and back of lift card

Procedure

1. Each student will create a workstation by covering the work area with butcher paper or other protective covering.
2. Use a fuming tank to fume an item with cyanoacrylate ester (at instructor's discretion). *Caution*: do not overfume the item. *Warning*! Do not inhale fumes; always properly vent the tank before removing the item.
3. With a fingerprint brush, apply powder to the item to develop fingerprints.
4. Lift developed prints with lifting tape.
5. Deposit prints on lifting card.
6. Affix the lifting cards to the Fingerprint Card Area and provide the requested information.
7. Complete the Post Lab Questions.

FIBERGLASS BRUSH

FINGERPRINT CARD AREA

Powder Type: Fumed: Yes   No
Surface Type:
Comments:

FINGERPRINT CARD AREA

Powder Type: Fumed: Yes   No
Surface Type:
Comments:

FIBERGLASS BRUSH

FINGERPRINT CARD AREA

Powder Type: Fumed: Yes   No
Surface Type:
Comments:

```
+------------------------------------------+
|                                          |
|                                          |
|                                          |
|                                          |
|          FINGERPRINT CARD AREA           |
|                                          |
|                                          |
|                                          |
|                                          |
+------------------------------------------+
```

Powder Type: Fumed: Yes   No
Surface Type:
Comments:

MAGNETIC BRUSH

```
+------------------------------------------+
|                                          |
|                                          |
|                                          |
|                                          |
|          FINGERPRINT CARD AREA           |
|                                          |
|                                          |
|                                          |
|                                          |
+------------------------------------------+
```

Powder Type: Fumed: Yes   No
Surface Type:
Comments:

FINGERPRINT CARD AREA

Powder Type: Fumed: Yes   No
Surface Type:
Comments:

MAGNETIC BRUSH

FINGERPRINT CARD AREA

Powder Type: Fumed: Yes   No
Surface Type:
Comments:

+---+

FINGERPRINT CARD AREA

+---+

Powder Type: Fumed: Yes   No
Surface Type:
Comments:

CAMEL HAIR BRUSH

+---+

FINGERPRINT CARD AREA

+---+

Powder Type: Fumed: Yes   No
Surface Type:
Comments:

FINGERPRINT CARD AREA

Powder Type: Fumed: Yes   No
Surface Type:
Comments:

CAMEL HAIR BRUSH

FINGERPRINT CARD AREA

Powder Type: Fumed: Yes   No
Surface Type:
Comments:

```
┌─────────────────────────────────────────────────────┐
│                                                       │
│                                                       │
│                                                       │
│                  FINGERPRINT CARD AREA                │
│                                                       │
│                                                       │
│                                                       │
└─────────────────────────────────────────────────────┘
```

Powder Type: Fumed: Yes   No
Surface Type:
Comments:

FEATHER BRUSH

```
┌─────────────────────────────────────────────────────┐
│                                                       │
│                                                       │
│                                                       │
│                  FINGERPRINT CARD AREA                │
│                                                       │
│                                                       │
│                                                       │
└─────────────────────────────────────────────────────┘
```

Powder Type: Fumed: Yes   No
Surface Type:
Comments:

FINGERPRINT CARD AREA

Powder Type: Fumed: Yes   No
Surface Type:
Comments:

FEATHER BRUSH

FINGERPRINT CARD AREA

Powder Type: Fumed: Yes   No
Surface Type:
Comments:

```

                    FINGERPRINT CARD AREA



```

Powder Type: Fumed: Yes   No
Surface Type:
Comments:

Post Lab Questions

1. What is the scientific name for superglue fuming?
2. What is the purpose of superglue fuming?
3. List all items necessary to properly set up and conduct the superglue fuming process.
4. Describe the types of surfaces for which the superglue fuming technique would be used.
5. Describe each type of fingerprint brush used. Discuss the benefits and drawbacks of each type of brush.

9-2: Fluorescent Powder Processing

Objectives

- Explain how an alternate light source is used for the development of fingerprints.
- Describe how light is converted to fluorescence.
- Practice developing prints with fluorescent powder.

Materials

- Writing utensil
- Digital camera (SLR preferably), if developed prints are to be photographically documented
- Macro lens (or diopters), if developed prints are to be photographically documented
- Tripod, if developed prints are to be photographically documented

Concept Overview

Light is a valuable tool in crime scene investigation. Without adequate illumination of a crime scene, an investigation is compromised because evidentiary items will not be seen and therefore not collected. There is no rival to clean white light in its ability to assist with searching for and visualizing evidence.

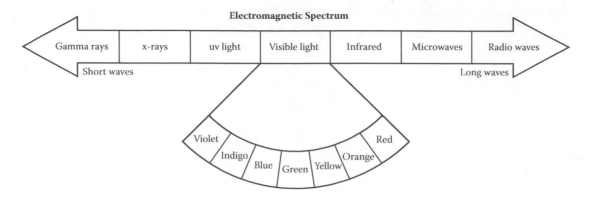

Figure 9.5
Electromagnetic spectrum

Visible light is radiant energy that we see all around us in the form of colors. However, it is a very small portion of all the radiant energy represented on the electromagnetic spectrum. Radiant energy travels in waves known as electromagnetic waves; the various forms of radiant energy are characterized by their wavelengths: short, medium, and long. Thus the electromagnetic spectrum is a continuum on which wavelengths of energy are arranged by their length. The electromagnetic spectrum includes gamma rays, x-rays, ultraviolet (UV) energy, visible light, infrared (IR) energy, microwaves, and radio waves (Figure 9.5).

Due to wavelength size, the nanometer (one billionth of a meter) is used to express the wavelength value or the length between the peaks of a wavelength of UV light, visible light, and IR light (Figure 9.6). Interestingly, there is an inverse relationship between wavelength and energy. The shorter the wavelength, the greater the energy; the longer the wavelength, the less energy present.

Generally, there are four actions that occur, separately or collectively, when light energy strikes an object. Two of those actions are *absorption* and *reflection*. When light energy strikes an object, it does so inclusive of all its primary colors: red, orange, yellow, green, blue, indigo, violet. The object will absorb or take in the majority of the wavelengths striking it and reflect or reemit wavelengths. For example, identifying grass as green occurs because the grass has reflected energy wavelengths defined as the color green and absorbed all other wavelengths or colors. When all wavelengths of light are reflected, the color identified is white. When all wavelengths of light are absorbed, the color identified is black. When light can pass through an object, *transmission* is occurring. Transparent objects such as water and glass are examples through which transmission of a particular wavelength or color can be observed. *Conversion* occurs when a wavelength is changed to another wavelength of different length. An example of this is luminescence, which is the ability to emit light without the origin of heat, such as light or chemicals. Luminescence is a broad term that includes phosphorescence and fluorescence. Phosphorescence occurs when an object is stimulated by light, retains the received radiation, and after removal of the stimulation, continues to visibly glow or give off light in the wavelength in which it was

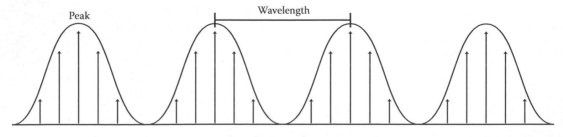

Figure 9.6
Electromagnetic wave.

converted. Fluorescence occurs when an object absorbs a stimulating light and converts it to a lower intensity (energy) and longer wavelength than that of the illuminating source. The resulting fluorescent light will differ in color from the stimulating light and emit a glowing appearance only during stimulation.

Fluorescence is a valuable tool in the development of friction ridge impressions. Fluorescent powders and dye stains are routinely used to process substrates for the development of these types of impressions. To properly process substrates through fluorescence, specific equipment is needed. An alternate light source (ALS) is a device that allows a specific wavelength of radiant energy to be emitted and used for the examination and processing of substrates. A portion of the emitted energy is reflected by substrates while some is absorbed. The absorbed energy excites the object's electrons into a higher electronic state. When these electrons return to their original state, energy is emitted that is lower in intensity with a longer wavelength, ergo fluorescence. When employing an ALS, the choice of wavelength is critical as different objects will absorb light and fluoresce at different wavelengths. Thus, a processor should view a substrate with multiple wavelengths to determine which will allow maximum fluorescence of the substrate and minimum fluorescence of the substrate's background. To view the fluorescence of an object, the processor must wear barrier glasses or use a barrier shield to view the object. The use of glasses or shields is imperative as they block out all wavelengths except that of the resulting fluorescent light. Barrier glasses or shields are of three colors: orange, yellow, and red. The decision as to which color to use is contingent upon the wavelength of light used. There are various combinations of wavelengths and barrier colors; the combination that provides optimal visualization is the desired combination, and this decision is based on training and experience.

The application of fluorescent powder, conventional and magnetic, is mechanically the same as the application of nonfluorescent powders. However, care needs to be taken with fluorescent powder as it tends to coat substrates quickly and heavily, thus obscuring developed prints. When using nonmagnetic powder, the feather brush is preferred over the fiber brush, because the feather brush does not acquire as much powder on its bristles and in turn applies less powder to a substrate than a fiber brush. When using magnetic powder, the created brush, or bulb of powder, at the end of the wand should barely glide over the substrate to minimize deposition of powder. An advantage to using a magnetic powder and applicator is the ability to clean the wand to prevent contaminating multiple powder colors. When using a fiber or feather brush, the brushes must be dedicated to one specific color to prevent contamination of both the powder and the brush with multiple colors. To properly process an item with fluorescent powder, the processor should be in a dimly lit area and must:

- Wear a set of barrier glasses or look through a barrier filter.
- Situate an ALS (or UV light) so the light emits on the substrate.
- Powder the substrate with the barrier and light in place (Figure 9.7).

As with nonfluorescent powder techniques, substrates may be fumed with cyanoacrylate ester (CA) prior to powdering to stabilize the print.

To document prints developed with fluorescent powder, they must be photographed. The manner in which the print was developed (i.e., the wavelength of light and color barrier filter used) is also the manner in which photographic documentation is to be obtained. The components and characteristics used to develop and view the print are the same ones needed for the camera to capture the image as the eye sees it (Figure 9.8).

These images are examination-quality photographs, meaning they will be submitted to an expert for examination, analysis, and scientific opinion. For these photographs, a macro lens or diopters (magnification lenses) are used in conjunction with a scale to capture the print in a 1:1 or life-size image. In manual mode, the camera should be set to ISO400 with the f/stop at f/11. The shutter speed should be properly adjusted for the lighting conditions of the photography area. Refer to the camera's exposure level scale. Typically, the indicator should be set to 0 for the initial image and then bracketed photographs should be taken. However, because fluorescent photography differs from photography using visible light, the exposure level scale should be set to −2 as a starting point. Photographs should then be bracketed around this value. In addition, the camera should be mounted on a tripod for stabilization, the frame should be filled with the print, and a cable release cord

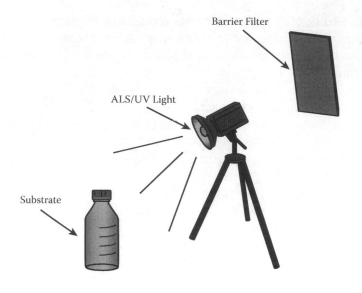

Figure 9.7
Visualizing fluorescent prints

or the camera's timer should be used to prevent camera shake or blur. Prior to capturing the image, it must be ensured that the camera lens is perpendicular or 90 degrees to the print. This will prevent creating image distortion. Prints developed with fluorescent powder may also be lifted with clear lifting tape and black lifting cards. Black lifting cards are used to create optimal visualization of the lifted colored print. Caution should be exercised after lifting fluorescent prints. It is possible that the lifting card will appear blank or void of a print. An ALS or UV light and barrier filter or glasses will allow the print to be visualized. This underscores the importance of identifying the lift as a fluorescent powder lift. Without the knowledge of the processing method, the lift card may be considered blank and thus lacking in evidentiary value. The processing method should be part of the following documentation required of all latent lifts:

- Name of processor
- Date/time
- Location from which the print was collected (object/substrate)
- Offense, case number, or title information provided by instructor

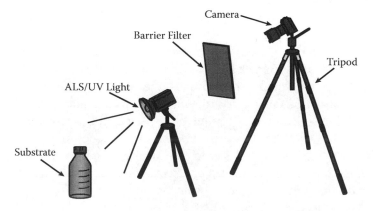

Figure 9.8
Photographing fluorescent prints.

A diagram must also be created on the back of the card. The diagram depicts the object that was processed, and an X is placed on the diagram to illustrate the location on the object from which the print was collected. On the front of the card (print side), an arrow is drawn to indicate the orientation of the print.

Procedure

1. Create a workstation by covering the surface work area with butcher paper or similar protective covering.
2. Ensure the following equipment has been gathered and ready for use:

   - ALS/UV light
   - Barrier filter/glasses
   - Fluorescent powder
   - Powder applicator (appropriate for either conventional or magnetic powder)
   - Lifting cards (black)
   - Clear lifting tape

3. Ensure the substrates have latent prints or apply them to the substrates.
4. Put on gloves and barrier glasses and arrange ALS/UV light so that it emits light on the substrate.
5. Load the applicator with powder and apply it to the substrate. Lightly process to avoid overpowdering.
6. Developed prints should be photographed, if desired by instructor. The same equipment and settings used to develop the prints will be used to photograph them, including a camera on a tripod. A properly captured image will:

   - fill the frame
   - maximize depth of field
   - include a scale

   For capture of fluorescent prints, bracketing will ensure an optimal image capture. Viewing the exposure level scale, capture images at −2, −1, and 0.
7. Lift the developed prints with lifting tape and place on lifting cards. Place proper documentation on lift card, and note that the print was developed with fluorescent powder.
8. Affix the lifting cards to the Fingerprint Card Area and provide the requested information.
9. Complete the Post Lab Questions.

FIBERGLASS BRUSH

FINGERPRINT CARD AREA

Powder Type: Fumed: Yes   No
Surface Type:
ALS/Barrier combination:

FINGERPRINT CARD AREA

Powder Type: Fumed: Yes   No
Surface Type:
ALS/Barrier combination:

FIBERGLASS BRUSH

FINGERPRINT CARD AREA

Powder Type: Fumed: Yes   No
Surface Type:
ALS/Barrier combination:

FINGERPRINT CARD AREA

Powder Type: Fumed: Yes   No
Surface Type:
ALS/Barrier combination:

MAGNETIC BRUSH

FINGERPRINT CARD AREA

Powder Type: Fumed: Yes   No
Surface Type:
ALS/Barrier combination:

FINGERPRINT CARD AREA

Powder Type: Fumed: Yes   No
Surface Type:
ALS/Barrier combination:

MAGNETIC BRUSH

FINGERPRINT CARD AREA

Powder Type: Fumed: Yes   No
Surface Type:
ALS/Barrier combination:

FINGERPRINT CARD AREA

Powder Type: Fumed: Yes   No
Surface Type:
ALS/Barrier combination:

FEATHER BRUSH

FINGERPRINT CARD AREA

Powder Type: Fumed: Yes   No
Surface Type:
ALS/Barrier combination:

FINGERPRINT CARD AREA

Powder Type: Fumed: Yes   No
Surface Type:
ALS/Barrier combination:

FEATHER BRUSH

FINGERPRINT CARD AREA

Powder Type: Fumed: Yes   No
Surface Type:
ALS/Barrier combination:

```



                    FINGERPRINT CARD AREA



```

Powder Type: Fumed: Yes   No
Surface Type:
ALS/Barrier combination:

Post Lab Questions

1. What are the advantages and disadvantages of the various ALS methods?
2. When should fluorescent powder be used?
3. How is the application of fluorescent powder different from the application of nonfluorescent powder?
4. Why is it important to use a proper combination of filter and barrier?

9-3: Fingerprint Development on Adhesive Tape: Crystal Violet

Objectives

- Understand the development reaction of crystal violet.
- Develop good techniques for processing adhesive tape with crystal violet.
- Practice developing prints on adhesive tape with crystal violet.

Materials

- Writing utensil
- Digital camera, if developed prints are to be photographically documented
- Scale of reference, if developed prints are to be photographically documented

Concept Overview

Crystal violet, also referred to as gentian violet, reacts to sebaceous lipids, commonly found in epithelial cells, by staining the area a deep purple color. Crystal violet works best on fresh prints. Substrates utilized should be nonporous or adhesive as porous items will absorb the dye stain with no visualization of prints. The liquid solution is easily created using crystal violet powder dissolved into a liquid solution. Documentation of prints developed via this method is through photography.

Procedure

1. Create a workstation by covering your area with butcher paper or other protective covering.

2. Using scissors, cut pieces of provided tape approximately 1.5 to 2 inches long. Lay these pieces, adhesive side up, on wax paper on your workstation.

3. On each piece of tape, apply fingerprints to the adhesive side and fold a small piece of the tape over onto itself to create a tab. (The tab will be used when moving the tape with tweezers.)

4. Use a fuming tank to fume the tape with cyanoacrylate ester. (At instructor's discretion.)

5. Before processing tape with crystal violet, put on:
   - Gloves
   - Chemical glasses
   - Apron or clothing protection

6. Ensure your workstation has the following before proceeding:
   - Tweezers
   - Glass or plastic bowl containing enough crystal violet to submerge a piece of tape
   - Glass or plastic bowl for capturing runoff water during rinsing of the substrate
   - Squeeze bottle containing tap water
   - Wax paper (to lay processed tape on)
   - Precut pieces of adhesive tape (with latent prints on adhesive side and a small folded tab for maneuvering with tweezers)

7. Use tweezers to place a piece of precut adhesive tape in the container of crystal violet.

8. Keep the tape submerged for 30 seconds to 1 minute.

9. Remove the tape with the tweezers and hold the tape over a second container. Using a squeeze bottle of tap water, rinse the reagent from the tape.

10. Examine the tape for developed prints. If no prints were developed, repeat the processing procedure. If prints were developed but are faint, repeat the processing procedure. Processing may be repeated until the desired contrast is achieved.

11. When the desired contrast is achieved, lay the tape, adhesive side up, on the wax paper for drying. Continue processing with subsequent pieces and types of tapes.

12. Document the developed prints with photography (if desired by instructor). A properly captured image will:
   - Fill the frame
   - Maximize depth of field
   - Include a scale

13. Preserve the developed prints by placing the *dry* tape, adhesive side up, on an index card. Anchor a piece of clear fingerprint tape on the index card approximately ¼ inch from one of the long sides of the tape. Use your finger to smooth the tape over the developed print and cut the tape. The index card should now preserve the tape and its developed print. Affix the lifting cards to the Fingerprint Card Area and provide the requested information.

14. Complete the Post Lab Questions.

Crystal Violet		
Tape Type	Fumed: Yes/No	Notes
1		
2		
3		
4		

1
Index card area

2

Index card area

3

Index card area

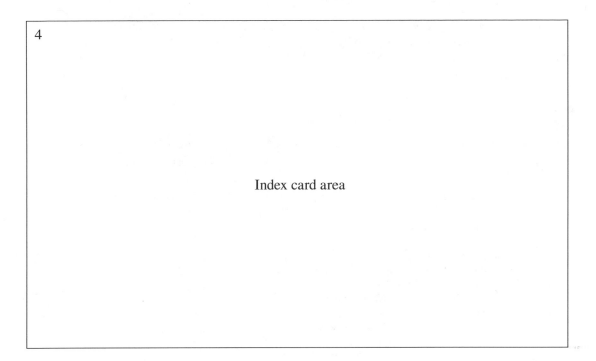

4

Index card area

Post Lab Questions

1. Were the prints easy to develop?
2. In reviewing the prints developed, how many prints are visible?
3. What are some challenges encountered when processing with crystal violet?

9-4: Fingerprint Development on Adhesive Tape: Sticky-side Powder

Objectives

- Understand the development reaction of Sticky-side Powder.
- Develop good techniques for processing adhesive tape with Sticky-side Powder.
- Practice developing prints on adhesive tape with Sticky-side Powder.

Materials

- Writing utensil
- Digital camera, if developed prints are to be photographically documented
- Scale of reference, if developed prints are to be photographically documented

Concept Overview

Sticky-side Powder is a silver metallic like substance that is combined with a detergent and water to create a paste substance. It reacts to the sebaceous and lipid components of fingerprint deposits through the development of gray or silver colored prints. Substrates utilized should be nonporous, as porous items will absorb the reagent with no visualization of prints. Documentation of prints developed via this method is through photography.

Procedure

1. Create a workstation by covering your area with butcher paper or other protective covering.

2. Using scissors, cut pieces of provided tape approximately 1.5 to 2 inches long. Lay these pieces, adhesive side up, on wax paper on your workstation.

3. On each piece of tape, apply fingerprints to the adhesive side and fold a small piece of the tape over onto itself to create a tab. (The tab will be used when moving the tape with tweezers.)

4. Before processing tape with Stick-yside Powder, put on
   - Gloves
   - Apron or clothing protection

5. Ensure your workstation has the following before proceeding:
   - Tweezers
   - Glass or plastic bowl containing Sticky-side Powder reagent
   - Camel hair brush
   - Glass or plastic bowl for capturing runoff water during rinsing of the substrate
   - Squeeze bottle containing tap water
   - Wax paper (to process tape on and lay processed tape on)
   - Precut pieces of adhesive tape (with latent prints on adhesive side and a small folded tab for maneuvering with tweezers)

7. Use tweezers to place a piece of precut adhesive tape on the wax paper.

8. Use the camel hair brush to "paint" the reagent on the adhesive side of the tape. Allow the reagent to remain on the tape for 30 to 60 seconds.

9. Use the tweezers to hold the tape over a second container. Using a squeeze bottle of tap water, rinse the reagent from the tape.

10. Examine the tape for developed prints. If no prints were developed, repeat the processing procedure. If prints were developed but are faint, repeat the processing procedure. Processing may be repeated until the desired contrast is achieved.

11. When the desired contrast is achieved, lay the tape, adhesive side up, on the wax paper for drying. Continue processing with subsequent pieces and types of tapes.

12. Document the developed prints with photography (if desired by instructor). A properly captured image will:
    - Fill the frame
    - Maximize depth of field
    - Include a scale

13. Preserve the developed prints by placing the *dry* tape, adhesive side up, on an index card. Anchor a piece of clear fingerprint tape on the index card approximately ¼ Inch from one of the long sides of the tape. Use your finger to smooth the tape over the developed print and cut the tape. The index card should now preserve the tape and its developed print. Affix the lifting cards to the Fingerprint Card Area and provide the requested information.

14. Complete the Post Lab Questions.

Sticky-Side Powder	
Tape Type	Notes
1	
2	
3	
4	

1
Index card area

2

Index card area

3

Index card area

4

Index card area

Post Lab Questions

1. Were the prints easy to develop?
2. In reviewing the prints developed, how many prints are visible?
3. What are some challenges encountered when processing with Sticky-side Powder?
4. Compare and contrast crystal violet and Sticky-side Powder.

9-5: Fingerprint Development on Absorbent Substrates: Iodine

Objectives

- Understand the development reaction of iodine.
- Develop good techniques for processing absorbent substrates with iodine.
- Practice developing prints on absorbent substrates with iodine.

Materials

- Writing utensil
- Heating element, such as an iron
- Digital camera, if developed prints are to be photographically documented
- Scale of reference, if developed prints are to be photographically documented

Concept Overview

Iodine reacts to the fatty and oily components of fingerprint deposits. Developed fingerprints are yellow-brown in color. Substrates processed may be porous or nonporous. Iodine is typically used on paper items, especially thermal paper. It also can develop prints on both sides of thermal paper, unlike ninhydrin, which will cause thermal paper to turn black and obscure developed prints. Iodine works best on fresh prints. Although this method is effective, it is important to note that iodine-developed prints fade rapidly. Documentation of developed prints, through photography, must be done quickly to ensure the maximum quality of print is being recorded and preserved.

Iodine may also be used in sequential processing, if desired. Iodine is the first processing method used followed by ninhydrin.

It is also important to note that a number of safety risks are involved with this method. Caution should be taken, especially when using iodine fuming tubes in which the processor blows through the tube, creating heat and moisture, to the iodine crystals located at the bottom of the tube. Much safer methods of processing include placing iodine crystals in a resealable bag with the item that needs to be processed or impregnating a silicon gel pack with iodine fumes and lightly brushing over the item in question.

Procedure

1. Create a workstation by covering your area with butcher paper or other protective covering.

2. Use scissors to cut substrates (paper/cardboard/raw wood) to fit inside fuming resealable bags.

3. Touch all substrates to deposit fingerprints.

4. Wear the following personal protection equipment:
   • Gloves
   • Mask
   • Eye protection
   • Apron or clothing protection

5. Ensure your workstation has the following before proceeding:
   • Tweezers
   • Iodine fuming wand or iodine crystals
   • Plastic, resealable bag (to contain the crystals and substrates)
   • Absorbent substrates (paper, cardboard, raw wood)
   • Access to a vent hood or well ventilated area

6. If using a fuming wand, follow the kit instructions and proceed to step 9.

7. If processing with iodine crystals, use tweezers to place absorbent substrates in a resealable bag containing the crystals.

8. Monitor the development of prints on the substrates. (The resealable bag should be placed on a covered or protected surface to prevent fume staining. Also, the bag should be in a vent hood or well-ventilated area during the sublimation of the crystals.)

9. When prints are developed, remove the substrates from the resealable bag and document them with photography, if desired by the instructor, before the prints fade. If fading occurs prior to documentation, the substrate(s) may be processed again. A properly captured image will:
   • Fill the frame
   • Maximize depth of field
   • Include a scale

10. Complete the Post Lab Questions.

Post Lab Questions

1. What surface types are conducive to iodine fuming?
2. Why is it important to wear personal protective equipment when processing with iodine?
3. How does iodine differ from other fingerprinting methods?
4. What are the advantages of using iodine fuming?

9-6: Fingerprint Development on Absorbent Surfaces: Ninhydrin

Objectives

- Understand the development reaction of ninhydrin.
- Develop good techniques for processing absorbent substrates with ninhydrin.
- Practice developing prints on absorbent substrates with ninhydrin.

Materials

- Writing utensil
- Digital camera, if developed prints are to be photographically documented
- Scale of reference, if developed prints are to be photographically documented

Concept Overview

Ninhydrin reacts to the amino acids and proteins of fingerprint deposits through the development of purple-colored prints. Substrates utilized for this process should be porous. This process works best on old prints. The substrate must have time to absorb the deposited amino acids. Over time, the developed prints will fade. Documentation of prints developed via this method is through photography. The shelf life of this reagent is approximately twelve months. Ninhydrin may used in sequential processing, if desired, after the application of iodine.

Ninhydrin may be purchased as an aerosol or in premixed liquid form as heptane based, methanol based, and acetone based from forensic vendors. Various application methods may also be used based on the item in question. Spraying, immersing, and painting or brushing are all acceptable methods of application.

Procedure

1. Before processing substrates with ninhydrin, put on
   - Gloves
   - Mask
2. Use tweezers to hold a substrate that has been prepared in advance with fingerprint deposits.
3. Apply the ninhydrin in a vent hood or well-ventilated area.
4. Allow prints to develop overnight or use an acceleration method. (Steam and heat from an iron may be used as an acceleration method to develop prints quickly. The key to this method is the application of the heat or steam without the iron contacting the substrate.)
5. Examine the substrate for developed prints.
6. Document the developed prints with photography (if desired by instructor). A properly captured image will:
   - Fill the frame
   - Maximize depth of field
   - Include a scale
7. Complete the Post Lab Questions.

Post Lab Questions

1. Compare and contrast the chemical processing methods for developing fingerprints.
2. Which chemical processing method provided more detail?
3. What surface type yielded the best chemically processed prints?
4. Is there one perfect chemical method for field work? Why or why not?

9-7: Print Development with Small Particle Reagent

Objectives

- Identify the component of print deposits with which small particle reagent (SPR) reacts.
- Describe the process of developing prints with SPR.
- Practice developing prints with SPR.

Materials

- Writing utensil
- Digital camera, if developed prints are to be photographically documented
- Scale of reference, if developed prints are to be photographically documented

Concept Overview

SPR is a micropulverized powder suspended in a solution. It is a liquid fingerprint powder that reacts with the fatty deposits of fingerprint residue. Initially, this reagent was used for the development of prints on wet surfaces. However, field and lab use has demonstrated the reagent's ability to develop prints on a variety of porous and nonporous substrates such as cardboard, plastic, vinyl, rocks, wood, and glass. It can also be used on substrate surfaces containing contaminant residues that would destroy a fingerprint brush. Documentation of the developed prints should be with photography followed by lifting with clear lifting tape.

Procedure

1. Create a workstation by covering your area with butcher paper or other protective material. This material should also be placed on the floor in your workstation area to catch spills and spatter.
2. Confirm the substrates to be processed have latent prints. If necessary, apply prints to your substrates.
3. Before processing with SPR, put on
   - Gloves
   - Apron or clothing protection
4. Ensure your workstation has the following supplies:
   - SPR in spray bottle (fine mist setting for adjustable nozzles)
   - Water in spray bottle
   - Tweezers
   - Heat-resistant dishes (two as capture containers for SPR and water runoff)
   - Substrates (with latent prints)

5. For applicable substrates, use reflective lighting from the light source of the work area to visualize latent prints on the substrate.

6. For practice developing prints on wet objects, wet the substrate prior to application of SPR.

7. Hold the substrate, either by hand or tweezers, over a heat-resistant dish and spray SPR above visualized latent prints. If no prints were visualized via reflective lighting, spray SPR at the top of the object to allow the reagent to run down the object. Do not spray SPR directly on the print(s); allow the solution to wash over the print(s).

8. After print development, move the object over a second capture container. Spray water onto the substrate, above developed prints, to rinse off the SPR. Reapplication is acceptable to achieve desired contrast.

9. Document the developed prints with photography (if desired by instructor). A properly captured image will:
   - Fill the frame
   - Maximize depth of field
   - Include a scale

10. Preserve the developed print through lifting. Lifting may be done with traditional lifting tape and backing card after the object has dried. (Allow the object or print to dry naturally; do not apply artificial heat.) A wet lift may also be conducted. This will require clear lifting tape, rubber squeegee, and a backing card. Ideally, two people should participate in a wet lift as the tape will not adhere to a wet surface; an assistant is needed to stabilize the object and anchor the tape. From the anchor point, use the squeegee to move across the tape over the print to push out water. Then, anchor one end of the tape on a backing card and use the squeegee to apply the tape to the card. (Prints developed on porous surfaces such as paper or cardboard will not be lifted.)

11. Repeat steps 5 through 10 for all objects provided by the instructor.

12. Affix the lifting cards to the Fingerprint Card Area and provide the requested information.

13. Complete the Post Lab Questions.

1

Backing card area

Object: Porous   Nonporous
Observations:

2

Backing card area

Object: Porous   Nonporous
Observations:

3

Backing card area

Object: Porous   Nonporous
Observations:

4

Backing card area

Object: Porous   Nonporous
Observations:

5

Backing card area

Object: Porous   Nonporous
Observations:

6

Backing card area

Object: Porous   Nonporous
Observations:

7

Backing card area

Object: Porous   Nonporous
Observations:

8

Backing card area

Object: Porous   Nonporous
Observations

9

Backing card area

Object: Porous   Nonporous
Observations:

10

Backing card area

Object: Porous   Nonporous
Observations:

Post Lab Questions

1. How many prints were developed using single particle reagent?
2. Based on your data table, which surface was the most successful?
3. What is single particle reagent?

9-8: Impression Casting: Dental Stone

Objectives

- Understand the applicability of dental stone as a casting medium.
- Develop good techniques for casting impressions.
- Practice casting impressions.

Materials

- Writing utensil
- Digital camera, if impressions are to be photographically documented
- Tripod, if impressions are to be photographically documented
- Off-the-camera flash or flood light for oblique lighting, if impressions are to be photographically documented
- Scale of reference, if impressions are to be photographically documented

Concept Overview

Impression evidence is extremely valuable as it can link the source of the impression to the location of impression (i.e., a crime scene). It is this affirmative link that compels the investigator to properly document it and collect it. Impression evidence can be discovered in two forms: two-dimensional and three-dimensional impressions. Two-dimensional impressions are used when the deposit of a substance onto a surface does not leave an indentation. Evidentiary samples are created when a substance, such as blood, dirt, oil, and so forth, is acquired on a medium and deposited onto nongiving surfaces such as tile, linoleum, or wood. Three-dimensional impressions are those that remain after an object has deformed the surface. In regards to shoes, this type of impression is generally found outdoors in mediums such as sand, dirt or soil, or snow.

The documentation of impression evidence is through photography. When photographing impressions, a tripod is necessary to stabilize the camera and position the camera perpendicular (90 degrees) to the impression. Oblique (side) lighting is the lighting technique utilized to maximize the use of shadows within the impression to enhance its detail. Oblique lighting is achieved when a light source (off-the-camera flash or flood light) is held several feet away from the impression at an angle of 45 degrees or less. A series of at least three images are taken of each impression with oblique lighting. The arrows in Figure 9.8 indicate the direction and location of the light source for each image series.

While these images are captured, the only moving variable is the light source. The camera does not move from its original position on the tripod. Further, the camera's timer or a cable release cord should be used to activate the camera rather than physically touching the camera and introducing camera shake. Camera shake will produce a blurry image.

Because these photographs may be examined by an impression expert, the images captured should be examination-quality photographs. As such, ISO100 should be used for maximum quality if enlargements are made; f/11 should be used to maximize depth of field; the shutter speed is not imperative as the camera is stabilized on a tripod. Further, the impression should fill the frame, and a scale should be included.

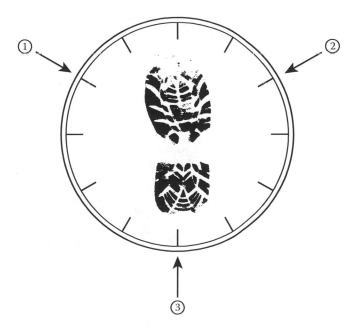

Figure 9.9
Lighting positions when photographing impressions.

Procedure

1. Place substrate (sand, dirt) into a disposable pan.

2. Create a footwear or tire impression in the medium.

3. Photograph the impression, if desired by the instructor, before casting. The equipment needed will be:
   - Digital camera
   - Tripod
   - Off-the-camera flash or flood light for oblique lighting
   - Scale of reference
   - Cable release cord or camera timer function
   The camera settings will be manual setting, ISO100, f/11, and shutter speed will be dictated by the camera's exposure level scale. A properly captured image will:
   - Fill the frame
   - Maximize depth of field
   - Include a scale

4. Mix the casting medium according to one of the following ratios to a consistency of pancake batter:
   - 2 lb dental stone + 9 oz water
   - $2\frac{1}{2}$ lb dental stone + 11–12 oz water

5. Pour the medium *into* the impression from one of the ends of the impression. Do not pour the medium *on top of* the impression as the weight of medium could destroy impression detail.

6. Allow the medium to set and dry for at least 3 to 4 hours before attempting to lift. Take care when lifting to avoid breakage. The cast will continue to dry and cure for the following 48 hours.

7. Complete the Post Lab Questions.

Post Lab Questions

1. Why is the consistency of the dental stone important?

2. Why is it important to photograph an impression before casting?

3. Can impression evidence be classified as class, individual, or both?

4. Why is it important to have both photographs and casts of an impression?

9-9: Impression Casting: Mikrosil

Objectives

- Understand the applicability of Mikrosil as a casting medium.
- Develop good techniques for casting impressions with Mikrosil.
- Practice casting impressions with Mikrosil.

Materials

- Writing utensil
- Digital camera, if impressions are to be photographically documented
- Tripod, if impressions are to be photographically documented
- Off-the-camera flash or flash light for oblique lighting, if impressions are to be photographically documented
- Scale of reference, if impressions are to be photographically documented

Concept Overview

Impression evidence is extremely valuable as it can link the source of the impression to the location of impression (i.e., a crime scene). It is this affirmative link that compels the investigator to properly document and collect it.

The documentation of impression evidence is through photography. When photographing impressions, a tripod is necessary to stabilize the camera and position the camera perpendicular (90 degrees) to the impression. Oblique (side) lighting is the lighting technique utilized to maximize the use of shadows within the impression to enhance its detail. Oblique lighting is achieved when a light source (off-the-camera flash or flash light) is held several feet away from the impression at an angle of 45 degrees or less.

Because these photographs may be examined by an impression expert, the images captured should be examination-quality photographs. As such, ISO100 should be used for maximum quality if enlargements are made; f/11 should be used to maximize depth of field; the shutter speed is not imperative as the camera is stabilized on a tripod. Further, the impression should fill the frame, and a scale should be included.

Mikrosil is a silicone casting material used to cast impression evidence such as tool marks and fingerprint impressions on textured surfaces. The casting medium is sold as a kit through forensic vendors. The kit includes Mikrosil, a hardener, a mixing pad, and a wooden stick for mixing the compound.

Procedure

1. Examine the tool-mark impression evidence on the substrates presented by the instructor.
2. Document the impression(s) with photography (if desired by instructor). The equipment needed will be:
   - Digital camera
   - Tripod
   - Off-the-camera flash or flash light for oblique lighting
   - Scale of reference
   - Cable release cord or camera timer function

   The camera settings will be manual setting, ISO100, f/11, and shutter speed will be dictated by the camera's exposure level scale. A properly captured image will:
   - Fill the frame
   - Maximize depth of field
   - Include a scale
3. Mix and apply the Mikrosil compound as follows:
   - Squeeze the Mikrosil tube to release the desired amount in a straight line on the mixing pad.
   - In a parallel line next to the Mikrosil, release the hardener from its tube so that it is the same length as the Mikrosil.
   - Use the wooden utensil to mix the two components.
   - After mixing, use the utensil as a tool to spread the Mikrosil compound over the impression.
   - Allow the compound to dry for 5 to 10 minutes.
   - Lift the dry medium and flip it over to see the cast impression.
   - Preserve the cast by placing it on an index card, impression side up, and use clear fingerprint tape to tape it to the card.
   - Affix the lifting cards to the Fingerprint Card Area and provide the requested information.
4. Complete the Post Lab Questions.

Mikrosil

Index card area

Substrate Type:
Comments:

Index card area

Substrate Type:
Comments:

Post Lab Questions

1. Compare and contrast Mikrosil and dental stone.
2. Which process was easier to use?
3. After using both methods, which process showed the most detail?
4. If too much hardener is added to the Mikrosil mix, what will happen?

Works Cited

Gardner, Ross M. *Practical Crime Scene Processing and Investigation.* Boca Raton, FL: CRC Press, 2005.

Houck, Max M., and Jay A. Siegel. *Fundamentals of Forensic Science.* San Diego, CA: Academic Press, 2009.

James, Stuart H., and Jon J. Nordby. *Forensic Science: An Introduction to Scientific and Investigative Techniques.* 3rd ed. Boca Raton, FL: CRC Press, 2009.

Lightning Powder Company, Inc. *Crystal Violet Technical Note.* April 2000. www.redwop.com (accessed March 1, 2011).

———. *Ninhydrin Technical Note.* April 2000. www.redwop.com (accessed March 1, 2011).

———. *Small Particle Reagent Technical Note.* April 2000. www.redwop.com (accessed March 1, 2011).

Robinson, Edward M. *Crime Scene Photography.* San Diego, CA: Elsevier, 2007.

Chapter 10

Advanced Techniques for Scene Processing

Key Terms

Angle of impact
Area of convergence
Area of origin
Drip pattern
Transfer pattern
Wipe pattern
Swipe mark
Spatter pattern
Expiratory spatter
Cast-off pattern
Arterial pattern
Splash pattern
Fly spots
Void pattern
Phenolphthalein
Tetramethylbenzidine (TMB)
O-tolidine
Hemastix

Learning Outcomes

1. Define bloodstain pattern analysis.
2. Understand the nature of bloodstains.
3. Recognize the various categories and subcategories in which bloodstains can be classified.
4. Understand the importance of determining directionality and impact angle.

10-1: Determining Directionality of Bloodstains

Objectives

- Understand the nature of bloodstains in flight.
- Recognize directionality characteristics of bloodstains.
- Practice determining the directionality of bloodstains.

Materials

- Writing utensil

Concept Overview

Bloodstain pattern analysis is a scientific discipline in which blood evidence and bloodstain pattern evidence are examined to determine the nature of the event(s) that occurred. Location of the bloodstain pattern evidence is a critical element as well as identifying the following characteristics of the blood drops: *size*, *shape*, and *distribution*.

Bloodstain size is a result of an inverse relationship involving the amount of force applied to a blood source. The greater the amount of force applied, the smaller the bloodstains. For example, when a blood source is impacted by a projectile from the explosive force of a discharged firearm, the preponderance of the bloodstains in the resulting bloodstain pattern is approximately 1 mm or less in size. When a blood source is impacted with a bludgeoning instrument, such as a pipe or bat, in motion from manual human force, the preponderance of the bloodstain size in the resulting bloodstain pattern is 1 mm to 4 mm in size. Bloodstain size is indicative of the nature of the force used in bloodletting events. It must be stressed, however, that a *single* bloodstain cannot be used to conduct an analysis of a scene. Bloodstain *patterns* are examined and analysis is conducted within the context of the entire scene, not within a vacuum of bloodstain evidence only.

When bloodstains are in flight, they travel in a parabolic arc while under the influence of gravity and affected by their own mass. The heavier they are, the farther they will travel. Bloodstains travel upward until the peak of their parabolic arc is reached, and then they fall downward out of their arc until the bottom of the arc is reached. If bloodstains are allowed to travel in their arcs unimpeded, the resulting shape of the bloodstain upon landing will be circular. If a bloodstain strikes a surface while in flight, the shape of the stain will be the angle at which it was in flight upon impact. Thus, the geometry of a bloodstain defines its *angle of impact*. Resulting characteristics of a bloodstain after impact on a surface can also indicate the *directionality* of the bloodstain. These characteristics include scallops, satellite stains, and tails. They are visible on the side of the stain opposite the side that impacted the surface. Examination of bloodstain directionality can assist in assessing the origination of the stain.

Distribution relates to bloodstain *patterns*, not solitary bloodstains. Examination of a bloodstain pattern may assist in determining which object created the stains, a common area of convergence, or the location of the blood source upon forceful impact.

It must be noted that the surface texture on which bloodstains land and bloodstain patterns result is the single most limiting factor related to bloodstain pattern analysis. For example, with the variables of blood drop volume, distance fallen, and force applied to blood (gravity at 90 degrees) the same, a bloodstain landing on a hard, smooth, nonporous surface would look very different from one landing on a rough, nonporous surface. The stain on the smooth surface would be circular in shape, while the stain on the rough surface would appear distorted and irregularly shaped.

Procedure

1. Examine the figures in the *Evaluation Worksheet*.
2. For each bloodstain, indicate its directionality by drawing an arrow parallel with the stain.
3. In the area provided, explain and support your determination via the visible characteristics of the stain.
4. Complete the Post Lab Questions.

Evaluation Worksheet

Stain 1

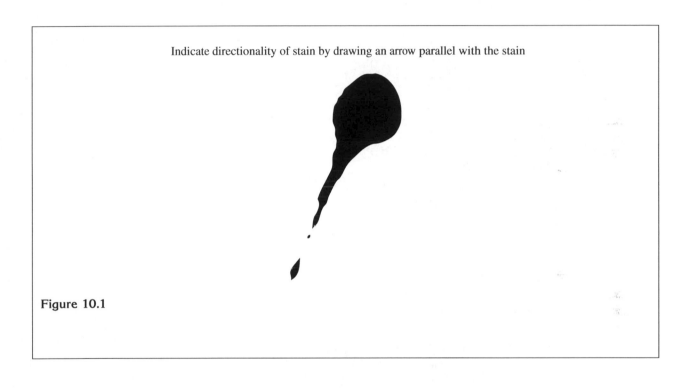

Indicate directionality of stain by drawing an arrow parallel with the stain

Figure 10.1

Support for determination of directionality:_____

_____

_____

_____

Stain 2

Indicate directionality of stain by drawing an arrow parallel with the stain

Figure 10.2

Support for determination of directionality: _____

_____

_____

_____

Stain 3

Indicate directionality of stain by drawing an arrow parallel with the stain

Figure 10.3

Support for determination of directionality: _____

_____

_____

_____

Stain 4

Indicate directionality of stain by drawing an arrow parallel with the stain

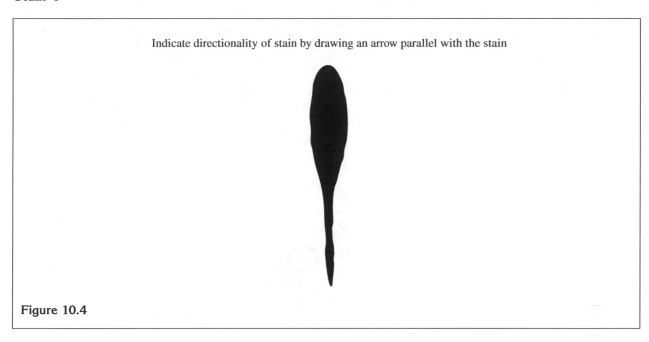

Figure 10.4

Support for determination of directionality:_____

_____

_____

_____

Stain 5

Indicate directionality of stain by drawing an arrow parallel with the stain

Figure 10.5

Support for determination of directionality:_____

_____

_____

_____

Stain 6

Indicate directionality of stain by drawing an arrow parallel with the stain

Figure 10.6

Support for determination of directionality:_____

_____

_____

_____

Post Lab Questions

1. How do satellite stains and scallops differ?
2. Why is understanding the directionality of the stain important?
3. What does the discipline of bloodstain pattern analysis encompass?
4. Why can't a single blood stain be used for analysis?

10-2: Determining Angle of Impact

Objectives

- Describe the method of measuring bloodstains.
- Practice calculating the angle of impact of bloodstains.

Figure 10.7
Ellipse of bloodstain, excluding scallops

Materials

- Writing utensil
- Scientific calculator

Concept Overview

Bloodstain pattern analysis is a scientific discipline in which blood evidence and bloodstain pattern evidence are examined to determine the nature of the event(s) that occurred. Location of the bloodstain pattern evidence is a critical element as well as identifying the following characteristics of the blood drops: *size*, *shape*, and *distribution*.

Bloodstain size is a result of an inverse relationship involving the amount of force applied to a blood source. The greater the amount of force applied, the smaller the bloodstains. For example, when a blood source is impacted by a projectile from the explosive force of a discharged firearm, the preponderance of the bloodstains in the resulting bloodstain pattern is approximately 1 mm or less in size. When a blood source is impacted with a bludgeoning instrument, such as a pipe or bat, in motion from manual human force, the preponderance of the bloodstain size in the resulting bloodstain pattern is 1 mm to 4 mm in size. Bloodstain size is indicative of the nature of the force used in bloodletting events. It must be stressed, however, that a *single* bloodstain cannot be used to conduct an analysis of a scene. Bloodstain *patterns* are examined and analysis is conducted within the context of the entire scene, not within a vacuum of bloodstain evidence only.

Figure 10.8
Ellipse of bloodstain, excluding tail

When bloodstains are in flight, they travel in a parabolic arc while under the influence of gravity and affected by their own mass. The heavier they are, the farther they will travel. Bloodstains travel upward until the peak of their parabolic arc is reached, and then they fall downward out of their arc until the bottom of the arc is reached. If bloodstains are allowed to travel in their arcs unimpeded, the resulting shape of the bloodstain upon landing will be circular. If a bloodstain strikes a surface while in flight, the shape of the stain will be the angle at which it was in flight upon impact. Thus, the geometry of a bloodstain defines its *angle of impact*. Resulting characteristics of a bloodstain after impact on a surface can also indicate the *directionality* of the bloodstain. These characteristics include scallops, satellite stains, and tails. They are visible on the side of the stain opposite the side that impacted the surface. Examination of bloodstain directionality can assist in assessing the origination of the stain.

Distribution relates to bloodstain *patterns*, not solitary bloodstains. Examination of a bloodstain pattern may assist in determining which object created the stains, a common area of convergence, or the location of the blood source upon forceful impact.

It must be noted that the surface texture on which bloodstains land and bloodstain patterns result is the single most limiting factor related to bloodstain pattern analysis. For example, with the variables of blood drop volume, distance fallen, and force applied to blood (gravity at 90 degrees) the same, a bloodstain landing on a hard, smooth, nonporous surface would look very different from one landing on a rough, nonporous surface. The stain on the smooth surface would be circular in shape, while the stain on the rough surface would appear distorted and irregularly shaped.

After the ellipse area has been established (Figures 10.7 and 10.8), the width and length are measured. These values are plugged into the formula given below to calculate the angle of impact for the stain. This value will always be less than 1. (If the value is greater than 1, the formula was transposed (L/W) prior to calculation.)

a. Width/Length = N
b. Inverse sine of N = impact angle

Example calculation:

W = 1
L = 3

a. 1/3 = 0.33
b. Inverse sine of 0.33 = 19 degrees

Although the mathematics used to derive an angle of impact is precise, the variables that affect a blood drop in flight preclude such accuracy for the determined impact angle. Thus, a derived angle within a range of 5 to 7 percent of the true angle is considered accurate.

Procedure

1. The data table in the *Evaluation Worksheet* provides the width and length for designated bloodstains. Using the provided formula and a scientific calculator, use the width and length values to calculate the angle of impact.

2. Complete the *Evaluation Worksheet*.

3. Complete Post Lab Questions.

Evaluation Worksheet

	Width (W)	Length (L)	W / L Value	Angle of Impact
Stain 1	1 mm	4 mm		
Stain 2	2 mm	3 mm		
Stain 3	1 mm	2 mm		
Stain 4	2 mm	6 mm		
Stain 5	4 mm	7 mm		
Stain 6	3 mm	4 mm		
Stain 7	4 mm	4.5 mm		
Stain 8	1.5 mm	4 mm		
Stain 9	3 mm	6.5 mm		
Stain 10	1 mm	1 mm		

a. Width / Length = N
b. Inverse sine of N = impact angle

Post Lab Questions

1. What three characteristics should be noted in regard to bloodstains?
2. What is the parabolic arc in regard to blood evidence? Why is it important?
3. How accurate is the angle of impact?
4. Name three variables that could affect the interpretation of bloodstain patterns.
5. Why are scallops, satellite stains, and tails not included in the mathematical calculation?

10-3: Creation and Analysis of Impact Angles

Objectives

- Create bloodstains with differing impact angles.
- Practice measuring bloodstains.
- Practice calculating the angle of impact of bloodstains.

Materials

- Writing utensil
- Scientific calculator

Concept Overview

Bloodstain pattern analysis is a scientific discipline in which blood evidence and bloodstain pattern evidence are examined to determine the nature of the event(s) that occurred. Location of the bloodstain pattern evidence is a critical element as well as identifying the following characteristics of the blood drops: *size*, *shape*, and *distribution*.

Bloodstain size is a result of an inverse relationship involving the amount of force applied to a blood source. The greater the amount of force applied, the smaller the bloodstains. For example, when a blood source is impacted by a projectile from the explosive force of a discharged firearm, the preponderance of the bloodstains in the resulting bloodstain pattern is approximately 1 mm or less in size. When a blood source is impacted with a bludgeoning instrument, such as a pipe or bat, in motion from manual human force, the preponderance of the bloodstain size in the resulting bloodstain pattern is 1 mm to 4 mm in size. Bloodstain size is indicative of the nature of the force used in bloodletting events. It must be stressed, however, that a *single* bloodstain cannot be used to conduct an analysis of a scene. Bloodstain *patterns* are examined and analysis is conducted within the context of the entire scene, not within a vacuum of bloodstain evidence only.

When bloodstains are in flight, they travel in a parabolic arc while under the influence of gravity and affected by their own mass. The heavier they are, the further they will travel. Bloodstains travel upward until the peak of their parabolic arc is reached, and then they fall downward out of their arc until the bottom of the arc is reached. If bloodstains are allowed to travel in their arcs unimpeded, the resulting shape of the bloodstain upon landing will be circular. If a bloodstain strikes a surface while in flight, the shape of the stain will be the angle at which it was in flight upon impact. Thus, the geometry of a bloodstain defines its *angle of impact*. Resulting characteristics of a bloodstain after impact on a surface can also indicate the *directionality* of the bloodstain. These characteristics include scallops, satellite stains, and tails. They are visible on the side of the stain opposite the side that impacted the surface. Examination of bloodstain directionality can assist in assessing the origination of the stain.

Distribution relates to bloodstain *patterns*, not solitary bloodstains. Examination of a bloodstain pattern may assist in determining which object created the stains, a common area of convergence, or the location of the blood source upon forceful impact.

It must be noted that the surface texture on which bloodstains land and bloodstain patterns result is the single most limiting factor related to bloodstain pattern analysis. For example, with the variables of blood drop volume, distance fallen, and force applied to blood (gravity at 90 degrees) the same, a bloodstain landing on a hard, smooth, nonporous surface would look very different from one landing on a rough, nonporous surface. The stain on the smooth surface would be circular in shape, while the stain on the rough surface would appear distorted and irregularly shaped.

After the ellipse area has been established, the width and length are measured. These values are plugged into the formula given below to calculate the angle of impact for the stain. This value will always be less than 1. (If the value is greater than 1, the formula was transposed (L/W) prior to calculation.)

   a. Width/Length = N
   b. Inverse sine of N = impact angle

Example calculation:

W = 1
L = 3

   a. 1/3 = 0.33
   b. Inverse Sine of 0.33 = 19 degrees

Although the mathematics used to derive an angle of impact is precise, the variables that affect a blood drop in flight preclude such accuracy for the determined impact angle. Thus, a derived angle within a range of 5 to 7 percent of the true angle is considered accurate.

Procedure

To prepare for the exercise, butcher paper may be taped down with masking tape to protect the areas in which the experiments will be conducted. If poster board is being used, it should be cut to properly fit onto the clip boards (approximately 8 1/2 by 11).

Prior to beginning the exercise, the group should label each sheet of paper or poster board with:

- Group member names
- Date
- Exercise title
- Grade of the substrate (level, gentle slope, steep slope)
- Height of the application (12, 24, 36, 48, or 60 inches)

1. Determine the first substrate grade (level, gentle slope, steep slope).
2. Secure a piece of copy paper or poster board onto the clip board.
3. Load blood from the container into the pipette.
4. Drop four to six drops of blood on the paper from one of the predetermined heights (12, 24, 36, 48, or 60 inches). Use a tape measure to ensure precision.
5. Remove the exemplar from the clip board and set it aside to dry.
6. Repeat these steps for the remaining heights for this substrate grade.
7. When all exemplars have been created for this substrate grade (5), continue on to another grade.
8. Continue to create the exemplars for the last substrate grade. When complete, 15 exemplars will have been created.
9. Clean up work area and prepare for measuring bloodstains. Needed are a metric scale (preferably in millimeters), scientific calculator, and the *Data Worksheet* for this exercise.
10. Assemble the first set of exemplars created. Choose the best formed bloodstain from each exemplar and circle it.
11. Use the *Data Worksheet* during the following. Use a metric scale to measure the width and length of the bloodstains chosen. Then determine the W/L ratio and the angle of impact.
12. Repeat this process for the remaining two substrate grades.
13. Complete the Post Lab Questions.

Data Worksheet

	Height	Width	Length	W/L Ratio	Angle of Impact
Substrate Grade	12				
	24				
	36				
	48				
	60				
Substrate Grade	12				
	24				
	36				
	48				
	60				
Substrate Grade	12				
	24				
	36				
	48				
	60				

Post Lab Questions

1. Did the unknown stain match any of the exemplars created? Support your answer.
2. In regard to the bloodstains created on a gentle slope, how did the angle of impact change as the height increased?
3. What information can be derived from bloodstains?
4. Can blood spatter alone solve a crime?

Optional Exercise

Unknown

Sample Number		Observations/Notes
Width/Length		
Width/Length Ratio		
Angle Ratio		

Based on the information obtained prior to testing the unknown, what height and grade were the unknown samples dropped from? Give specific details to support this conclusion.

10-4: Bloodstain Pattern Recognition and Identification

Objectives

- Explain the basis of taxonomy in bloodstain pattern analysis.
- Practice recognizing passive stains and dynamic patterns.
- Practice identifying bloodstain patterns.

Materials

- Writing utensil

Concept Overview

Bloodstains and blood stain patterns are examined and analyzed for their characteristics. It is via these observed characteristics that they are classified or placed in a taxonomic structure. The underlying basis of the taxonomy in bloodstain pattern analysis is the event or act that created the stains or patterns. Thus, the identification of a pattern necessarily defines the parameters of the event through which the resulting pattern occurred.

Within the classification system of bloodstain patterns, there are two basic categories: dynamic and passive. Dynamic patterns result when force impacts a blood source. Passive stains occur due to some action other than the involvement of force upon a blood source. Bloodstain patterns that do not meet the criteria for either passive or dynamic categories are placed in a miscellaneous category.

Bloodstain patterns are further subdivided into the pattern types. SWGSTAIN, the Scientific Working Group on Bloodstain Pattern Analysis which was created in 2002 by the FBI, defines the following categories as:

- Drip: A liquid that dripped into another liquid, at least one of which was blood.
- Transfer: Results from contact between a blood-bearing surface and another surface.
- Wipe: An altered bloodstain pattern resulting from an object moving through a preexisting wet bloodstain.
- Swipe: The transfer of blood from a blood-bearing surface onto another surface, with characteristics that indicate relative motion between the two surfaces.
- Spatter: Results from a blood drop dispersed through the air due to an external force applied to a source of liquid blood.
- Expiratory: Blood that is forced by airflow out of the nose, mouth, or a wound.
- Cast-off: Blood drops released from an object due to its motion.
- Projected (or arterial): Results from the ejection of a volume of blood under pressure.
- Splash: Results from a volume of liquid blood that falls or spills onto a surface.
- Fly spots: Minute stains that result from bloodstained flies landing on a substrate.
- Void: Absence of blood in an otherwise continuous bloodstain or bloodstain pattern.

Although these are main categories, it may be possible to further subcategorize the patterns.

Once the observer can distinguish individual patterns within a scene and deduce, through their characteristics, the force classification, substantive theories may be developed concerning acts that may have been carried out at a scene.

Procedure

1. Examine the provided photographs.
2. For each photograph, determine its category: dynamic, passive, or miscellaneous.
3. For each photograph, identify the bloodstain pattern.
4. Provide support for your decisions in the *Data Worksheet*.
5. Complete the Post Lab Questions.

Data Worksheet

Photograph 1	Category: Dynamic, Passive, Miscellaneous	Pattern:
	Support:	

Photograph 2	Category: Dynamic, Passive, Miscellaneous	Pattern:
	Support:	

Photograph 3	Category: Dynamic, Passive, Miscellaneous	Pattern:
	Support:	

Photograph 4	Category: Dynamic, Passive, Miscellaneous	Pattern:
	Support:	

Photograph 5	Category: Dynamic, Passive, Miscellaneous	Pattern:
	Support:	

Photograph 6	Category: Dynamic, Passive, Miscellaneous	Pattern:
	Support:	

Photograph 7	Category: Dynamic, Passive, Miscellaneous	Pattern:
	Support:	

Photograph 8	Category: Dynamic, Passive, Miscellaneous	Pattern:
	Support:	

Photograph 9	Category: Dynamic, Passive, Miscellaneous	Pattern:
	Support:	

Photograph 10	Category: Dynamic, Passive, Miscellaneous	Pattern:
	Support:	

Post Lab Questions

1. How many of the stains were easily identified?
2. How do swipe patterns and wipe patterns differ?
3. What type of bloodstains are classified as dynamic?
4. Why is it important to view blood spatter evidence within a scene context?

10-5: Presumptive Tests

Objectives

- Understand the concept of presumptive tests.
- Recognize a positive and negative presumptive test.
- Practice using various types of presumptive tests.

Materials

- Writing utensil

Concept Overview

Chemical presumptive tests are one way in which crime scene personnel can test a substance that could possibly be blood. These tests rely heavily on chemicals that change color when they come in contact with the hemoglobin found in blood. To confirm the chemicals are working properly, conducting positive and negative controls is crucial. A positive control is a sample that is known to react with the test chemical. For the purpose of this exercise, a known blood sample should be used to obtain a positive result (i.e., the proper color change) before continuing. A negative control is a known sample that is clean or void of any blood-based substrate. This sample should yield no color change.

Although these tests effectively record negative blood results, positive results do not always equate to human blood. False positives, substances that contain the same chemical properties as the substance being tested, may be generated by chemicals, or the blood present may be animal blood instead of human blood. Further testing is needed to confirm the substance is human blood. There are several different types of presumptive tests that can be used.

A phenolphthalein test, also known as the Kastle-Meyer test, is commonly used in the field of forensic science. A reaction occurs when a blood stain comes in contact with hydrogen peroxide, producing a color reaction. The test area generally progresses from clear to pink, indicating the substance could be blood.

Another chemical presumptive test is the tetramethylbenzidine, or TMB, test. This is a catalytic test that is also based on peroxidase-like activity. Substances that come in contact with this chemical generally change from clear to a blue-green color when a positive reaction occurs.

O-tolidine is also a presumptive test that can be used to test for the presence of hemoglobin. It works in the same way as the phenolphthalein test, except the phenolphthalein is replaced with an o-tolidine stock solution. Substances that come in contact with this chemical generally change from clear to a blue-green color when a positive reaction occurs.

Hemastix are small reagent test strips that were originally designed to detect trace amounts of blood in urine. The small yellow square on the end of the test strip serves as the chemical basis for the test. Again, based on peroxidase-like activity, the yellow test square will turn blue-green in the presence of strong samples. Smaller or weaker amounts of sample may yield a reddish-orange color.

Presumptive tests are beneficial in aiding crime scene personnel in determining which substances are potential blood evidence and should be collected for subsequent analysis.

Procedure

1. Each student will create a workstation by covering the work area with butcher paper or other protective covering.
2. Using the materials provided, create samples as instructed by the instructor.
3. Test the samples using the presumptive tests provided.
4. Warning! Carefully follow the directions for each test as described by the manufacturer and your instructor.
5. Complete the *Data Worksheet*.
6. Complete the Post Lab Questions

Optional Exercise

1. Once the *Data Worksheet* has been completed, obtain an "Unknown" sample from the instructor.
2. Test the "Unknown" sample.
3. Complete the *Unknown Data Worksheet* and complete any follow-up questions.

Data Worksheet

PRESUMPTIVE TEST: _____

Sample	Reaction Time	Color Change	Observations

Data Worksheet

PRESUMPTIVE TEST: _____

Sample	Reaction Time	Color Change	Observations

PRESUMPTIVE TEST: _____

Sample	Reaction Time	Color Change	Observations

Data Worksheet

PRESUMPTIVE TEST: _____

Sample	Reaction Time	Color Change	Observations

Post Lab Questions

1. Which method was easier to use? Why?
2. Why are presumptive tests important?
3. Define the following: false positive, positive control.
4. Based on the concept overview, complete the following worksheet.

Presumptive Test	Color Change
TMB	
Hemastix	
Phenolphthalein	
O-tolidine	

Optional Exercise

Unknown

Sample Number		Observations/Notes
Presumptive Test Used		
Reaction Time		
Color		

Based on the information obtained prior to testing the unknown, what is the unknown sample? Give specific details to support this conclusion.

Works Cited

Analysis, Scientific Working Group on Bloodstain Pattern. *Recommended Terminology*. April 2009. http://www2.fbi.gov/hq/lab/fsc/backissu/april2009/standards/2009 04 standards01.htm (accessed March 1, 2011).

Gardner, Ross M. *Practical Crime Scene Processing and Investigations*. Boca Raton, FL: CRC Press, 2005.

James, Stuart H., and Jon J. Nordby. *Forensic Science: An Introduction to Scientific and Investigative Techniques*. 3rd ed. Boca Raton, FL: CRC Press, 2009.

Special Scene Considerations

Key Terms

Fire tetrahedron
Magnetometer
Ground penetrating radar
Stratification

Learning Outcomes

1. Recognize the components of the fire tetrahedron.
2. Understand the challenges associated with fire scenes.
3. Understand intrusive versus nonintrusive methods used at a burial site recovery.
4. Recognize the challenges associated with a burial site recovery.

11-1: Recovering Fingerprints from Burned Items

Objectives

- Describe the scene conditions at fire events that make fire scenes difficult and complex.
- Explain the meaning of fire tetrahedron.
- Practice recovering fingerprints from burned items.

Materials

- Digital camera, if recovered prints are to be documented through photography
- Scale of reference, if recovered prints are to be documented through photography
- Tripod, if recovered prints are to be documented through photography
- Photography log, if recovered prints are to be documented through photography

Concept Overview

Fire scenes are some of the most challenging scenes a crime scene technician may face. It is important for technicians to understand not only the concept of fire but also the dangers and trials that may be associated with this type of scene. An easy way of looking at the conditions necessary to start a fire is by viewing a fire tetrahedron. A fire tetrahedron is a representation of the elements that must be present for a fire to start. The components of a fire tetrahedron are a source of heat or energy such as a match, a fuel, and oxygen. A chain reaction occurs between the fuel and oxygen, when this reaction occurs the heat expedites the chemical reaction to the point of ignition. This chemical reaction can happen slowly or quickly, depending on the type of fuel used and the ignition temperature associated with it.

Fire scenes can be extremely difficult to process. A number of hazards and challenges exist, including structural instability, exposed metal, nails and other dangerous objects, inhalation hazards, and water damage to material at the scene. Lighting may also cause problems, making it difficult for crime scene personnel to see the crime scene properly.

Although many challenges exist, the recovery of fingerprints is still possible with the employment of the proper methodology. Although burnt items may be black from soot deposition, the process of burning has literally etched the fingerprint(s) into the exterior of the item. The challenge is to remove the soot in order to expose the fingerprint.

The first step in the process is visual examination. The processor must have access to clean white light for a proper examination. The item is manipulated by holding and handling the corners and edges so that all surface area is examined for visible prints or partial prints. If any prints are visible at this point, they should be documented with photography before attempting to remove any soot.

The second step involves the removal of soot from the substrate. If the substrate is heavily coated with soot, the item may be held under a gentle stream of running water. The substrate is once again visually examined for the presence of prints. Before continuing, allow the substrate to air dry. After the item has completely dried, the processor may use either lifting tape or a feather brush to remove the remaining layers of soot. The decision as whether to use tape or brush will depend on the condition of the substrate and the processor's experience. The removal process continues until prints are revealed or the original surface of the substrate is visible. This process is time consuming and requires tenacity and patience on the part of the processor. (If the item surface is not heavily coated with soot, the rinsing step may be omitted.)

The third step is documentation. Any prints uncovered must be photographed. Because the fingerprints have been etched into the substrate, the chance of a complete, successful lift is doubtful. Recall that a properly captured image will:

- Fill the frame
- Maximize depth of field
- Include a scale

If the prints are photographed, a photography log is an ideal tool to use.

Procedure

1. Create a workstation with butcher paper to protect surface of work area.

2. Visually examine the substrate provided by the instructor for prints. If prints are visualized, photograph them, if desired by the instructor. Recall that a properly captured image will:
   - Fill the frame
   - Maximize depth of field
   - Include a scale

3. Determine the condition of the substrate surface, notate as heavily or lightly soot covered.

4. Attempt to remove soot via one or several of the following methods:
   - Gently running water over surface (substrate should completely dry before using the subsequent methods)
   - Removal with lifting tape
   - Removal with feather brush

5. Continue the process of soot removal until prints are revealed or the original surface of the item is visible.

6. Document prints with photography, if desired by the instructor. Use a photography log if prints are photographed.

7. Complete the Post Lab Questions.

Photography Log

Activity:		Photographer:			
Date:		Location:			
Camera used:			Time start:		Time end:

Photo #	ISO	Aperture	Shutter Speed	Lens	Subject Description

Post Lab Questions

1. What are the components of the fire tetrahedron?
2. What are the challenges associated with fire scenes?
3. Why might lighting be a problem?
4. How do fingerprints survive the fire?
5. What techniques are used to remove soot from the object(s) containing fingerprints?

11-2: Burial Recovery

Objectives

- Describe nonintrusive methods of locating graves.
- Describe intrusive methods of locating graves.
- Practice recovering buried remains.

Materials

- Writing utensil
- Digital camera, if burial is to be documented through photography
- Scale of reference, if burial is to be documented through photography
- Tripod, if burial is to be documented through photography
- Photography log, if burial is to be documented through photography

Concept Overview

Burial recovery sites are challenging crime scenes to work due to various types of soil or exposure to the environment for an extended period of time. Generally law enforcement is presented with a burial site in one of two ways. One is when a citizen notifies the police of a found grave. An example would be a man out walking his dog stumbles upon a shoe sticking out of the ground and notifies the police. The second is when law enforcement is looking for a grave. This is often the case when a crime scene is discovered with no body or victim present. Suggestions at the scene lead law enforcement to believe there is a secondary scene and form a search of a specific area and locate a body.

When searching for a burial site, a number of nonintrusive methods may be employed. The first, and least invasive, is a visual search. A variety of factors may affect what a searcher may see, including disturbed soil or dirt, vegetation that has been disturbed or is redeveloping, or an abnormality in the soil or dirt. This abnormality can be seen as a high mound of soil when no others are present or as a deep depression in the soil when the elevation is otherwise consistent. Other nonintrusive methods include use of magnometers, ground-penetrating radar, and infrared thermography. Magnometers detect abnormalities in the surface's magnetic field. Metallic items are easily identified using this technique. Ground-penetrating radar (GPR) sends a low frequency signal into the ground, which is returned in different ways according to the condition it has encountered. Infrared thermography utilizes the heat signatures of the soil. Differences between soil in the surrounding area and the soil close to or at the site may help deduce where the burial site is located.

While nonintrusive methods are preferred, it is sometimes necessary to utilize intrusive methods. These include the use of probes and vapor monitors. Probes are used to detect the different densities within the soil. Teams are generally formed in the area and they implement standard searching techniques. Any detection of abnormality should be noted and further explored by the team leader. Vapor monitors are used to detect the gases associated with decomposition. Generally the vapor monitors are used in conjunction with another technique such as probing.

Once a site has been discovered, the surface debris should be removed. These items and areas can be excavated independent of the burial site. Loose debris, once documented, should be removed from the scene and evaluated for evidentiary significance. Ground plants should be removed by cutting them at the surface. Careful consideration must be taken not to disturb other layers of soil. Plants should never be pulled out of the ground. Screens are used to filter all soil removed from the site. This could help locate small items of interest such as small bones, teeth, bullets, and so forth. The actual excavation is conducted in levels. The excavation is generally conducted as an archeological site would be. Each layer, or stratification, is removed, approximately 2 inches at a time, evenly across the site before proceeding deeper into the grave. Each artifact located is in the reverse order of deposit into the grave. Shoveling soil arbitrarily from the grave will result in the loss of stratum where the evidence or object was located. This can make reconstruction of the scene difficult or impossible. As new artifacts are exposed, they should be carefully documented and mapped on the overlying grid. Initial exposure of the body is the apex of the search; however, protocol should not be ignored. Digging within the stratification should continue as normal until the entire body is exposed. Once the body has been documented, it can be removed from the grave by the proper personnel. While this seems a natural end, searchers should continue to excavate below the body for additional artifacts or evidentiary items of value to the case.

Burial sites are tedious and time-consuming investigation areas, but to conduct a site in haste could be detrimental to an investigation.

Procedure

1. Confirm who are the members of your excavation team and the role or task of each member. The duties in this exercise include:
   - Creating field notes
   - Excavating
   - Sifting removed soil
   - Collecting measurements for plotting evidence
   - Creating sketches
   - Documenting with photography (if desired by instructor)
2. Create a workstation by placing butcher paper over your work surface area.
3. Examine the burial site and begin a field note document. This document should contain:
   - Observations of the site
   - Description of the site
   - Recovered items, time of recovery
4. Use a measuring tape to determine the dimensions of the site, including the depth.
5. Excavate the site by removing one spoonful of dirt at a time and transferring it into a provided container. The removed dirt should be sifted for item recovery. Dirt removal should be the same depth across the entire site before continuing on to deeper depths.
6. If an item is revealed, plot the item using the grid or triangulation or rectangular coordinates on a grid method. These measurements will be used to create a projection sketch of the burial site. Also, record the depth of the recovered items; these measurements will be used to create an elevation sketch. (Choose one system of measurement for data collection.)
7. Use the provided mapping measurement records to record measurements.
8. Use the provided sketch canvases to sketch a cross-projection view and elevation sketch of the burial site.
9. Create a finished projection sketch of the burial site depicting the recovered items, if desired by the instructor.
10. Create a finished elevation sketch of the burial site depicting the recovered items, if desired by the instructor.
11. Complete the Post Lab Questions.

Mapping Measurement Record: Grid/Triangulation						
Sketch artist:			Date:			
Location:						
Object or Placard #	Object	RP-1	RP-2	RP-3	RP-4	Depth

Mapping Measurement Record: Grid/Rectangular Coordinates				
Sketch artist:		Date:		
Location:				
Object or placard #	Object	X measurement	Y measurement	Depth

Sketch Canvas

Sketch Canvas

Sketch Canvas

Sketch Canvas

Post Lab Questions

1. Describe two ways in which a burial site may be found.
2. Name two nonintrusive techniques that can be used at a burial site.
3. Name two intrusive techniques that can be used at a burial site.
4. Why is it important to cut plants or other vegetation at the surface of the grave?
5. Why is it important to keep digging once the body has been removed?

Works Cited

Gardner, Ross M. *Practical Crime Scene Processing and Investigations*. Boca Raton, FL: CRC Press, 2005.

Houck, Max M., and Jay A. Siegel. *Fundamentals of Forensic Science*. San Diego, CA: Academic Press, 2009.

James, Stuart H., and Jon J. Nordby. *Forensic Science: An Introduction to Scientific and Investigative Techniques*. 3rd ed. Boca Raton, FL: CRC Press, 2009.

12

The Role of Crime Scene Analysis and Reconstruction

Key Terms

Literature review
Scientific method
Hypothesis
Event analysis
Event segments
Absolute chronology
Relative chronology
Terminus ante quem
Terminus post quem
Terminus peri quem
Flow chart

Learning Outcomes

1. Understand the importance of journal articles.
2. Define scientific method.
3. Review and implement the components of an experimental design.

12-1: Journal Article Review

Objectives

- Increase technical vocabulary related to forensic science.
- Learn how to concisely summarize a journal article containing scientific and detailed information.
- Increase scientific knowledge base.
- Enhance critical thinking skills.

Materials

- Writing utensil

Concept Overview

Journal articles published in periodicals are documents pertaining to a specific subject matter. It is critical to read journal articles to keep up with new and advancing technologies within specific fields, especially forensic science.

A journal article is generally divided into several sections: abstract, introduction, materials and methods, results and discussion, and a conclusion. The abstract is generally a 200- to 600-word short description of the article. It is a quick reference for the reader containing key words and a few sentences regarding the overall concept. The introduction expands on the abstract and may cover background information such as previous studies or describe the novelty of the project. It also may contain a historical perspective on specific scientific techniques being used. The materials and methods section describes the items used in the experiment and the methods used to obtain data. Results and discussions depict data that have been generated, either positive or negative, and dialogue regarding the study's success or short comings. The conclusion gives an overall summary to the work being presented and possibly outlines future research or implications regarding the data or techniques used.

In regard to forensic science, a number of journals exist to keep crime scene technicians and scientist, up to date. Examples of the journals are *Journal of Forensic Science, Forensic Science International, Journal of Forensic Identification,* and the *Lone Star Forensic Journal.*

Procedure

1. Search for a forensic science journal article to review. During the review, provide the following in the *Evaluation Worksheet*:
   - Identify three terms with which you are not familiar. For each term, describe or define each and articulate how each is related to or used in the forensic science field.
   - Write a brief summary of each section of the article. Each section should be summarized in three to four sentences.
2. Prepare a paper for submission to your instructor.
3. Complete the Post Lab Questions.

Evaluation Worksheet

Term	Definition

Section	Summary
Introduction	
Material and Methods	
Results and Discussion	
Conclusion	

Post Lab Questions

1. Did you find the article interesting? Why or why not?
2. Was the article difficult to summarize? Why or why not?
3. List three things learned from reading the article.
4. Describe how reading the article could benefit you as a crime scene technician and/or forensic scientist.
5. Explain how the author could expand the article to be more beneficial or informative.

12-2: The Scientific Method

Objectives

- Learn the components of the scientific method.
- Design an experiment using the scientific method.

Materials

- Writing utensil

Concept Overview

Science is the understanding and processing of the systematic study of the structure and behavior of the physical and natural world through examination and testing. The actual process of science, known as the scientific method, involves taking an unknown "event" and proposing various plausible explanations for the event. Conclusions are drawn based on the data collected from experiments conducted to prove or disprove specific questions regarding the plausible explanations. These questions are used to form hypotheses, or neutral statements, which can either be proven or disproven.

In forming questions regarding scientific events, there are two characteristics that must be addressed. The first is that the questions that are asked must be *testable*. It is not scientific to ask, "How many leprechauns are at the end of a rainbow?" because a test cannot be created to answer the question. The second is *repeatability*. Science is a public venture and data are generally published for other scientists to review. It is important that other scientists in the field be able to replicate your work and gain comparable results. If only you can make a particular experiment work, it is not science.

After the hypothesis has been formed, it is necessary to generate data. The data must be carefully analyzed to either prove or disprove the hypothesis. This is known as the probative value.

When preparing an experiment using the scientific method, several areas should be addressed:

1. Title of the project: The title should address the focus of the project.
2. Defined problem or question: This is the overall objective of the research: what is to be proven and why.
3. Data collection: Identify what data need to be collected and the method of collection most beneficial to the research being conducted. This should also include a literature review of all articles relevant to the project. Upon review of data, it is important to determine whether the project has been done before and what makes this project unique.
4. Working hypothesis: The specific question(s) addressed within the project and the related testable expectation(s). These should be written as statements that can be proven or disproven.

5. Classification and organization of data: Data should be classified and organized logically and in a manner that facilitates experimentation. This area should also address the storage and disposal of data (i.e., biological samples) should it be necessary for the project.

6. Test of hypothesis: Explanation of the specific process or mechanism by which the hypothesis is to be tested.

7. Conclusion: A short summary describing why the research is important, who it will benefit from it, and literature points that support the statements made.

The scientific method has been used for many years. Undoubtedly, the proving or disproving of a hypothesis leads to hypotheses being formed and more research and scientific data analysis; therefore, many people view this as a circular process. Without this process, new advances and techniques could not be developed.

Procedure

1. Select a topic for research.
2. Complete the *Evaluation Worksheet.*
3. Complete the Post Lab Questions.

Evaluation Worksheet

Title of the Project:	Question/Problem
Collection of Experimental Data (Method of collection, number of samples, etc.)	Literature Review References 1. 2. 3.
Working Hypothesis (Statement that can be proven or disproven)	Data Organization (Dissemination of data, storage, disposal, etc.)
How will the hypothesis be tested? (Evaluation standards such as data with an error rate of less than 5 percent from which all the hypotheses can be proven)	Conclusion Summary Points 1. Why is the project important? 2. How is this project beneficial to the field? 3. Possible other projects/literature points to support statements.

Post Lab Questions

1. Was it difficult to find a topic of interest to you? What were some of the specific difficulties?
2. Why is the scientific method important?
3. Why is it important for your data to be reproducible for other scientists?
4. How is preparing an experimental scientific method beneficial?
5. Why is it important to stay current on topics, technologies, and techniques pertinent to the field of forensic science?

12-3: Flowcharting Event Segments

Objectives

- Describe event analysis.
- Describe how the chronology of event segments is defined.
- Explain why graphic representations of crime scene reconstruction are valuable.
- Practice flowcharting event segments of an incident.

Materials

- Writing utensil

Concept Overview

Crime scene reconstruction is the culmination of all previous activities. Its purpose is to try to establish the order or sequence of events that led to the incident. The incident is defined as the overall situation being investigated. Each event is a macrocomponent of the overall incident. The ability to reconstruct these individual events is vital to closing an investigation. In order to reconstruct a crime scene, a number of steps should be taken. The steps are:

1. Collect data and establish likely events: Collection begins at scene arrival. From the time crime scene personnel enter a scene, throughout the processing of the scene, and finally the scene debriefing, information is being collected.

2. Establish event segments from the data available: By reviewing and considering all information collected at the scene, crime scene personnel begin to define specific aspects of the reconstruction of the incident.

3. Define associated event segments: When these aspects are realized, event segments will emerge. It is then important to associate specific actions. A review should be conducted of all actions to ensure an important event has not been missed.

4. Order and sequence the associated event segments: Once the event segments have been identified, order and sequence of the segments must be established. Relative chronology articulates only the event segments in relation to one another. It identifies what precedes or follows a given set of actions and does not speak to absolute time. Segments are sequenced using the following terms:

   - Terminus ante quem: event segment(s) that has preceded another event segment

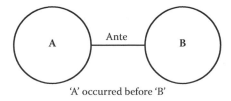

'A' occurred before 'B'

Figure 12.1
Ante quem

- Terminus peri quem: event segments that were likely simultaneous

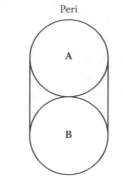

'A' and 'B' occurred simultaneously

Figure 12.2
Peri quem

- Terminus post quem: event segment(s) that has followed another event segment

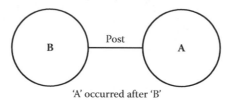

'A' occurred after 'B'

Figure 12.3
Post quem

5. Review the information: From beginning to end, the information used to form the event segments and subsequent sequencing must be checked and confirmed. Contradictory evidence may result in multiple crime scene reconstruction scenarios.

6. Determine the order of events: A certain level of assumption must be taken in order to begin the reconstruction process. Once all facts have been reviewed, a relatively clear picture of the events should emerge. The addition or consideration of new items of events or data in regard to the scene may help to better define the sequence or possibly eliminate data from the chart.

7. Flow chart the overall incident: The incident is now in the form of specific actions, ordered and sequenced as efficiently as the data from the scene will allow. In order to make the events visually clear to understand, either to other law enforcement personnel or to lay members of the court, a flow chart should be constructed. This allows those involved to easily see event segments that caused the incident.

As an example of the process, read the following passage, examine Table 12.1, and then see the Flowchart 1 (Figure 12.4).

A woman purchased rose bushes to plant alongside her house. The woman's dog could see her and the newly purchased bushes through the slats of the backyard fence. The dog barked and jumped wildly in excitement. Fearing her dog would damage the new roses, the woman did not allow her dog to leave the fenced backyard. After planting the bushes, the woman went inside her house. Shortly thereafter, a strong wind began to blow. Later in the afternoon, the woman returned outside to admire her new roses. She found several holes in the ground where she had planted the bushes. The door of her backyard fence was standing open. Walking through the fence door into the backyard, she saw mangled bushes on the ground, and her dog had a muddy snout and paws. As he walked toward her, she could see rose petals caught in his collar.

Table 12.1

Scene	Action	Sequence Number	Relative Chronology
Flower bed/exterior house	Flower bush planted	1	Ante quem
	Plants destroyed	3	Post quem
Backyard	Dog gets out of backyard/ open gate	2	Peri quem
	Mangled flowers found/dog muddy paws and snout	4	Post quem
Environment	Strong wind blows	2	Peri quem

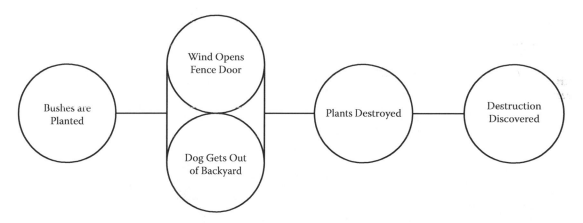

Figure 12.4
Flowchart 1

Procedure

1. Read the *Report of Events*.
2. Analyze the report, complete the *Data Worksheet* identifying the event segments or specific actions (see Figure 12.5).
3. Complete the flow chart.
4. Make a list of the identified event segments.
5. Fill in the provided Flowchart 2 (Figure 12.6) in a logical relative chronology.
6. Complete the Post Lab Questions.

Evaluation Worksheet

Report of Events:

A homeowner returned home to find her residence had been broken into. Responding investigators found that the south door of the residence was open and had pry marks along the side near the door knob, and one of the door's glass panes had been broken out. On the east side of the residence in the yard several feet away from a side door, there was an ice pick with what appeared to be blood on it. This side door was open with no apparent damage to it, but there was a red-colored liquid that appeared to be blood on the interior side of the door near the door knob. The side door was an entry/exit door of the den. On the den floor, several apparent bloodstains were visible. A trail of stains was between the den and master bedroom. In the master bedroom, there were apparent bloodstains on the floor, and a closed jewelry box was lying on its side on the bed. The white comforter near the jewelry box was marked with what appeared to be bloodstains. A half-eaten peanut butter cookie was also on the bed. In the remainder of the residence, the doors of the cabinets and dressers of each room were standing open. In the living room, the television was tuned to a music channel, and there was a half-eaten sandwich, an open bag of peanut butter cookies, and a partial glass of orange soda on the coffee table.

Scene	Action	Sequence Number	Relative Chronology
Den			
Bedroom			
Living Room			
Dining Room			
Kitchen			
Master Bedroom			
Garage			
Outdoors			
Environment			

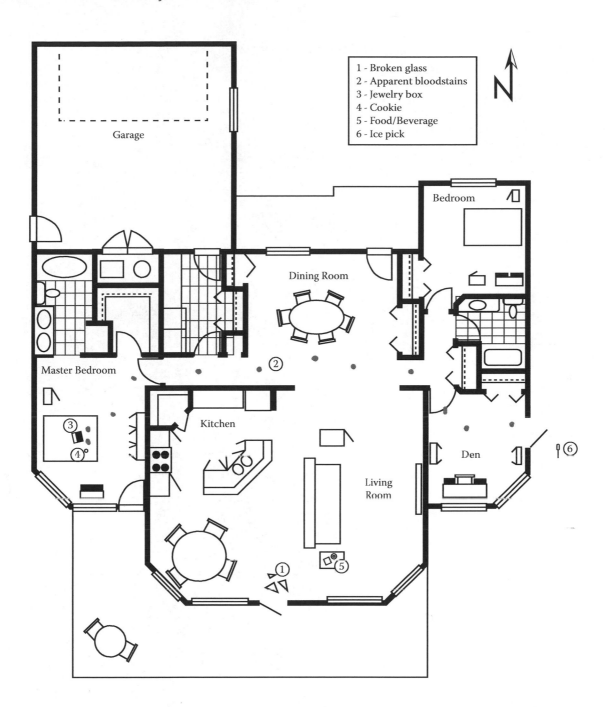

Figure 12.5 Scene diagram

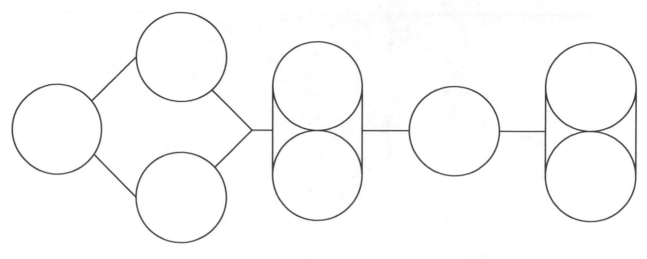

Figure 12.6 Flowchart 2

Post Lab Questions

1. Name the seven steps associated with crime scene reconstruction.
2. Why is crime scene reconstruction important?
3. Define the following terms: terminus peri quem, terminus post quem, terminus ante quem.
4. Give an example of when multiple crime scene reconstructions may be necessary.
5. Using the *Flow Chart Canvas*, complete a flow chart given the following information:

Scene	Action	Sequence Number	Relative Chronology
Living Room	Front door lock broken	1	Ante quem
	Footwear impressions exiting scene	3	Post quem
Kitchen	All cabinets open	2	Peri quem
Master Bedroom	All dresser drawers open/closet in disarray	2	Peri quem

Flow Chart Canvas

12-4: Crime Scene Investigation and Reconstruction

Objectives

- Practice crime scene investigation
- Practice crime scene reconstruction

Materials

- Writing utensil
- Digital camera
- Tripod
- Diopters (highly desirable)
- *Crime Scene Control Log* (created in Chapter 3 exercise)
- *Photography Log* (Chapter 6)
- *Field Note Document Template Outline* (created in Chapter 8 exercise)
- Scientific calculator (calculation of applicable blood evidence)
- Off-the-camera flash (highly desirable for three-dimensional impression photography)

Concept Overview

This exercise provides the opportunity to demonstrate the skills attained through conducting the exercises of this workbook. It is important to practice all components of crime scene analysis in order to become proficient in the techniques discussed in this workbook.

Procedure

This exercise provides the opportunity to investigate a mock crime scene and demonstrate the skills attained through conducting the exercises of this workbook.

1. After the instructor creates teams of four to five people, determine who will be the team leader.

2. The team leader will make duty assignments to include photographer, sketcher, evidence collector or processor.

3. The instructor will present a scene for your team to investigate. Tasks to carry out include:

   - Assessing the scene and defining the inner perimeter (and outer perimeter, if applicable) with barrier tape
   - Utilizing of a *Crime Scene Control Log*
   - Documenting the scene with a *Field Note Document Template Outline*
   - Documenting the scene via photography, using a *Photography Log*
   - Documenting the scene with rough and finished sketches
   - Processing collected evidence for friction ridge impressions
   - Photographing developed impressions, if desired by instructor

4. Review your notes, photographs, and evidence to conduct a scene reconstruction in the form of a flowchart. The flowchart should include specific actions of the scene, without supposition, presented in a logical sequence.

5. Each team member is responsible for submitting a supplement report that includes his or her assignment and actions at the scene and in the lab. The team leader is responsible for the in-depth scene report. Each team will submit a case file to the instructor that includes:

- Scene report and supplements
- Scene sketches: rough and finished (with necessary elements)
- Scene photographs: media card or thumbnail photos
- Evidence submission sheet (completed)
- Latent print lift card (with necessary elements)
- Flowchart

6. Each team will conduct a verbal case review of their scene for the class. Photographs must accompany the presentation. This may be via PowerPoint or photo viewer software.

Evidence Submission Sheet

Analysis Codes	
Trace = TR	Drugs = DR
Serological/DNA = DNA	Toxicology = TOX
Fingerprints = FP	Questioned = QD
Ballistics/Firearms/Tool marks = FA	

Item Number	Item Description	Analysis

Photography Log					
Activity:			Photographer:		
Date:			Location:		
Camera used:				Time start:	Time end:
Photo #	ISO	Aperture	Shutter Speed	Lens	Subject Description

Mapping Measurement Record: Baseline Coordinates				
Sketch artist:			Date:	
Location:				
Placard #	Object	Compass direction from baseline	X measurement	Y measurement

Mapping Measurement Record: Triangulation						
Sketch artist:				Date:		
Location:						
Placard #	R or IR	Object	RP-1	RP-2	RP-3	RP-4

Mapping Measurement Record: Rectangular Coordinates

Sketch artist: Date:

Location:

Placard #	Object	X measurement	Y measurement

Sketch Canvas

Sketch Canvas

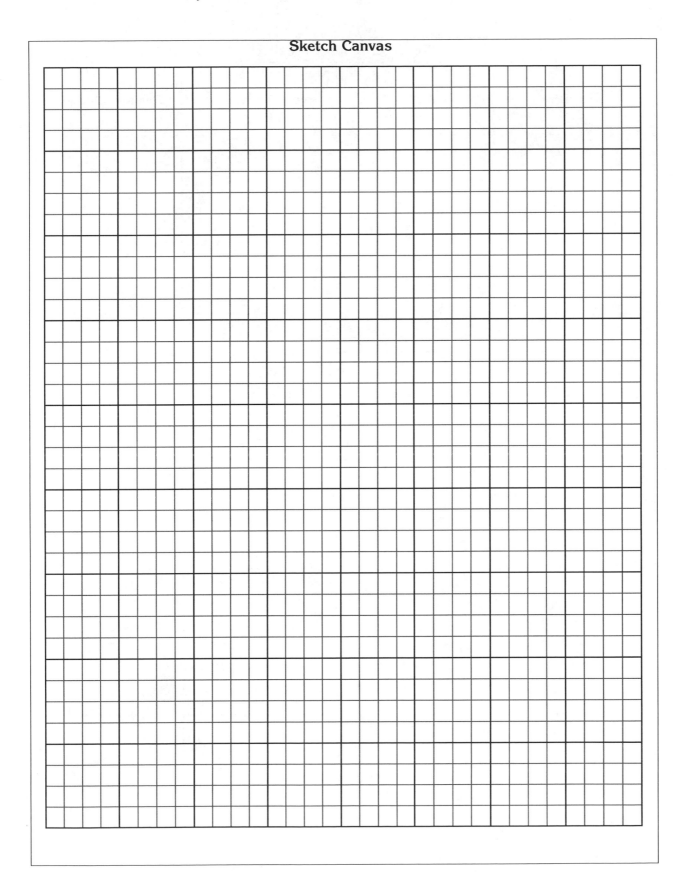

Reconstruction Worksheet			
Scene	Action	Sequence Number	Relative Chronology
Den			
Bedroom			
Living Room			
Dining Room			
Kitchen			
Master Bedroom			
Garage			
Outdoors			
Environment			

Flow Chart Canvas

Works Cited

Gardner, Ross M. *Practical Crime Scene Processing and Investigations*. Boca Raton, FL: CRC Press, 2005.

Houck, Max M., and Jay A. Siegel. *Fundamentals of Forensic Science*. San Diego, CA: Academic Press, 2009.

Index

A

ACE-V, 22, 25

B

Ballistics evidence. *See* Firearms/ballistics evidence
Biohazards, 47
Biological evidence. *See* Serological/DNA evidence
Bloodstain pattern analysis
    angle of impact, 150, 154, 155, 156, 158
    classification system, 161
    directionality, 150, 156
    distribution, 157
    ellipse area, 156, 158
    flight patterns, 150, 156, 158
    overview, 150, 157–158
    shape, 157
    size, 155, 157
    surface texture, 150, 158
    volume, drop, 156
Burial sites
    challenges of, 172, 173
    probes, 172
    searching for, 172
    surface debris, 173
    vapor monitors, 172–173

C

Chemical evidence, 13
    false-positive results, 28
    negative controls, 28
    positive controls, 28
    presumptive tests, 163–164
Circle search, 51, 52
Class characteristics of evidence, 12–13
Contamination of evidence, 13
Crime prevention, 5
Crime repression, 5
Crime scene control log, 33
Crime scene photography. *See* Photography, crime scene

Crime scenes. *See also* Burial sites; Fire scenes
    assessing, 38
    buffer zone, 46
    control log, *see* Crime scene control log
    decedent, condition of, 39
    documenting, 38, 39, 64–65
    environmental characteristics, 39
    investigative methodology, 39–40
    location, 39
    mapping, 74–75, 81, 86, 87
    measurement systems, 68, 69
    notes, *see* Notes, crime scene
    perimeter, establishing, 46
    photography, *see* Photography, crime scene
    primary focal point, 34–35, 46
    processing, 38, 46
    reconstruction, *see* Reconstruction, crime scene
    reports, *see* Reports, crime scene
    searching, 38, 51–52
    secondary scenes, 46–47
    sketching, 68, 74, 75, 80, 86
    uniqueness of, 39
Crystal violet, 125, 126
CSI, 5
CSI effect, 5
Cyanoacrylate ester fuming (CA fuming), 105, 106, 117

D

Data classification, 185
Digital single lens reflex (SLR) camera, 56, 58
DNA evidence. *See* Serological/DNA evidence
Drug analysis, 17

E

Electromagnetic spectrum, 116
Emergency care, 34
Emergency medical services (EMS), 34
English rules, 68

Printed and bound by PG in the USA